NATURAL LANGUAGE
FOR DEAF CHILDREN

Photo by Pach Bros.

Dear little child, this little book
Is less a primer than a key
To sunder gates where wonder waits
Your "Open Sesame!"

RUPERT HUGHES
With a First Reader

NATURAL LANGUAGE

FOR DEAF CHILDREN

By

MILDRED A. GROHT, D.Ped.
Academic Principal, Lexington School for the Deaf
New York City

With a Foreword by

CLARENCE D. O'CONNOR, M.A., L.H.D.
Superintendent, Lexington School for the Deaf

ALEXANDER GRAHAM BELL ASSOCIATION
FOR THE DEAF, INC.

Headquarters: The Volta Bureau   Washington, D. C.

Dedicated to deaf children everywhere in love, and in the hope that they may grow "in wisdom and stature, and in favour with God and man."

—Luke 2:52

FOREWORD

THE ABILITY OF MAN TO COMMUNICATE WITH HIS FELLOW MAN IS the major skill that differentiates him from animals. This priceless gift of language, which comes so easily to the majority of us who hear, is the open-sesame to the achievement of educational, vocational, social and civic competence so necessary for happy and effective living. Without this we would be mere animals moving about without the capacity to determine in any way our destiny on this earth.

For centuries the latter was the status of children born deaf. It was considered impossible to develop in them any language skills, and for this reason it was believed they could not be educated. As a result, they were traditionally accorded neither the privileges nor the responsibilities of citizenship, and usually were kept hidden from the public eye by their kindly, but helpless and hopeless parents.

The past several centuries have witnessed the gradual emancipation of the deaf from this status of neglect to the level of first class citizenship they may achieve today. The main ingredient in this emancipation is, of course, language, for this is the magic key that opens the doors to knowledge, understanding, and self-realization.

In our own country in the past century or more, many capable people have contributed ideas and techniques designed to increase the certainty of the acquisition by the deaf of as nearly normal communication skills as possible. Among these important contributions are a number of so-called "systems" of teaching language. Each of these has contributed in one way or another, and still contributes under certain circumstances, to the effective development of language ability in the deaf. However, each one, by the very nature of its formalism, implies that a deaf child must develop his ability to communicate in a different way than his hearing brothers and sisters. With the imposition of this limitation too exclusively and for too long a time it is inescapable that the language fluency of a deaf child so exposed cannot possibly equal or approach that of his hearing peers.

Dr. Groht, the author of this book, is one of America's most distinguished teachers of the deaf, particularly in the field of the communication arts. She has unceasingly expounded the philosophy that deaf children can acquire fluent use of English comparable

FOREWORD

to that of the hearing through what has come to be known as the "natural" method, and through her own skillful teaching of deaf children and guiding of teachers she has demonstrated that this can be done without question. Through her writings, her demonstrations, and her lecture courses, and now through the chapters of this excellent book, she has very generously passed on to her co-workers the benefits of her rich experience in this specialized field.

It has been my great privilege to have been associated with Dr. Groht at the Lexington School for twenty-seven years. I have the deepest devotion to her as a person and infinite respect for her as a teacher. It is with pride and confidence that I commend this book to all teachers of the deaf.

Clarence D. O'Connor
Superintendent, Lexington School for the Deaf

TABLE OF CONTENTS

Preface... xi

Acknowledgments.. xiii

Introduction.. xv

Chapter I   THE YOUNG CHILD AND LANGUAGE..... 1

Chapter II   THE FORMATIVE YEARS......................... 10

Chapter III GROWING IN AWARENESS...................... 20

Chapter IV LEARNING BY DOING............................. 36

Chapter V   NEW WORLDS TO EXPLORE................. 54

Chapter VI ESTABLISHING PATTERNS OF
SELF-EXPRESSION................................. 70

Chapter VII IMAGINATION ENRICHES EXPRESSION 86

Chapter VIII GROWING IN INDEPENDENCE.............. 103

Chapter IX FREEDOM OF EXPRESSION.................. 129

Chapter X   BROADER HORIZONS........................... 146

Chapter XI ON THEIR OWN................................... 157

Chapter XII A WILL—AND A WAY....................... 169

Appendix.. 185

PREFACE

THIS PREFACE IS WRITTEN PRINCIPALLY TO NOTE THAT THIS BOOK IS not in any sense of the word a course of study for teachers of the deaf, or an outline of language, or a curriculum of the language arts in a school for the deaf. It is a book about language and how best to fortify deaf children with the ability to use language in every phase of their lives.

It is my intent to give the reader an insight into the value and importance of language, to help him find better ways and means of teaching language to the deaf through a deeper understanding of words as a medium of communication in daily living, and to make suggestions for the development and use of natural language on the part of the deaf.

This book has been written at the behest of many teachers who have earnestly desired a better and surer way of giving their deaf pupils the ability to use language as hearing people use it—for communication, for thinking, for communing, for reasoning and for just plain pleasure. This desired and desirable approach has not been possible in many instances because the present available language workbooks and textbooks for the deaf have consisted of analytical drills and exercises. As a result, most deaf children and deaf adults have been given a stereotyped, parrot-like, and limited use of language—a language without spontaneity, naturalness or individuality. A system of language teaching that develops the memory, but not the mind, will not attain for the learner the ability to use the language most needful to him in each and every situation in which he finds himself.

It is my hope that this book will fulfill the wishes and needs of all those teachers who work with the deaf and who want to give them the utmost in knowledge and mastery of language. Through its use, these children will have the opportunity to lead happy, well-integrated and satisfying lives in a world made up of both deaf and hearing people—a world where the ability to communicate is a paramount necessity.

ACKNOWLEDGMENTS

It is with deep appreciation that I make known my sincere gratitude to—

—the Board of the Alexander Graham Bell Association for the Deaf and the Board of Trustees of the Lexington School for the Deaf for their assistance and encouragement in the preparation of this book.

—Dr. Clarence D. O'Connor for his unfailing interest, understanding and help and for all that the experience of working with him these many years has meant to me. He was at all times in total agreement with the philosophy underlying the natural method of teaching language to the deaf and gave me a free hand in experimenting and exploring all phases of language teaching. It is largely due to Dr. O'Connor's keen interest and pleasure in the language attainments of Lexington pupils that the school family functions with such accord and harmony in planning and carrying out our language program.

—Miss Alice Dunlap, former executive secretary of the Alexander Graham Bell Association for the Deaf, for her inestimable help in editing this book and above all for her unceasing prodding, which made the book take form and shape.

—Miss Minnie M. Hill, assistant executive secretary of the Association, whose inspiration, advice and counsel have done much to make this book possible, and to all members of the staff of the Alexander Graham Bell Association for their friendly interest and efforts in typing the manuscript and in assisting in the task of reference details.

—Miss Beatrice Ostern for her invaluable assistance in reading the manuscript, for her many suggestions, and for her help in assembling the material included in this book. Miss Ostern has contributed more than words can tell to the language program of the Lexington School because of her deep understanding of the language problems of the deaf and her ability to meet the problems intelligently.

—all of the members of the staff of the Lexington School who have creatively and effectively applied the philosophy implied in this book, and who have spared neither time nor effort in order to bring to fulfillment the ideas and the ideals, as well as the spirit, underlying the use of the natural method of teaching language to the deaf. My debt to each and every teacher is great indeed!

ACKNOWLEDGMENTS

Acknowledgment is also made to the following source for the quotation on page 157:

Flesch, Rudolf Franz (ed.), *The Book of Unusual Quotations.* New York: Harper & Brothers, 1957.

INTRODUCTION

It was the writer's privilege in the early years of her teaching to work with the deaf boys at a camp run by the late Dr. Samuel G. Davidson, who was for many years an instructor of language in the upper school of the Pennsylvania School for the Deaf at Mt. Airy. Dr. Davidson, who had become deaf at the age of thirteen, was widely known for his success in teaching English to the deaf. In an article entitled "Mental Development through Language Study," Dr. Davidson offered excellent advice on the teaching of language which, if it had been heeded, would have vastly improved the techniques used by many teachers of the deaf.[1] He wrote in part:

> I have been a special teacher of English for more than twenty years, yet I have never regarded English as the chief end of my work. I have taught language as a means of mental development and with the expectation, which has never been disappointed, that as the faculties are trained to higher efficiency, the difficulty of acquiring language is proportionately lessened—that where the medium of instruction is English, not the sign language, power of expression always keeps pace with growth in knowledge and the ability to think logically and fluently.
>
> . . . .
>
> . . . let the teacher always keep in mind that her work is to develop the faculties of her pupils through language, rather than to teach language itself. All her methods will then, naturally and almost automatically, be directed to this end. If, on the other hand, she thinks of language as a form study, her work will be formal, mechanical, lacking in interest, and ineffective as a means of developing either thought or language.
>
> . . . .
>
> Having a pupil read once, rapidly, a statement, a paragraph, or a story, so as to get the sense of it, and then reproduce it in his own language, will train him in quick perception of the relation of ideas to one another, and develop his memory for facts, while his incorporation of such of the language as has impressed itself upon him in this hurried reading, with such other language as he has previously acquired, is the best possible way to develop his powers of linguistic expression.

---

[1] All quotations of Dr. Samuel G. Davidson have been taken from "Mental Development Through Language Study," *American Annals of the Deaf*, 59: 113-117, March 1914.

INTRODUCTION

Having him study the same statement, paragraph or story over and over until the words are ground into his memory does not profit him as regards either language or mental growth. It weakens perception, the power of instantaneous recognition of relations, and the only form of memory that is of much real use —that which fixes things permanently in the mind from the first cognition of them.

.   .   .   .

In story work, questions that demand thought on the part of pupils, and the answers to which depend upon what is suggested rather than what is explicitly stated will do much to develop thought and language. On the other hand, questions which may be answered by merely repeating the language of the book are of little value either way.

An interesting observation by Dr. Davidson, that is as true today as it was when he made it, should not be left out of these quotations:

The kind of reading that one often finds in the children's page of school papers, and which is published as samples of the lessons the pupils are required to study, should be put under the same ban as cocaine, morphine, and other soporific drugs. You can very often trace the influence of such language work in the mental vacuity and incapacity of pupils in the higher grade. These children do not look upon nor use language as the expression of thought, but only as a string of words put together according to an established order and with sufficient correctness to satisfy the teacher.

Teachers of the deaf who would take time to go back over the history of the education of the deaf in the United States would be amazed to read of the forward-looking ideas of these very early educators—ideas that in later years were being heralded by the prominent leaders of progressive education and discussed as the "modern" approach. One has only to read some of the papers of Alexander Graham Bell, A. L. E. Crouter, S. G. Davidson, Sarah Fuller, David Green, Harris Taylor, Caroline Yale and many others, to discover that these early leaders in the field of the education of the deaf were far ahead of their times. Modern textbooks on the language arts often merely echo the truths fathomed long ago by those men and women. One wonders how it came about that teachers who followed them forgot about using the lives and the interests and needs of their deaf students as the focal point of language teaching—how they lost the understanding that mental growth and language achievement go hand in hand—how the deaf child's imagination and reasoning power could be developed through the use of language—how new language could be acquired through the process of association, and memory made keen through interest and understanding.

For what reasons did teachers forget to really *teach,* and in place of teaching try to pour a mass of unrelated language facts into the deaf child's head and be satisfied to receive them back from the child in parrot-like fashion? They *must* have known that this automatic performance had little or no lasting value to the child! In time, the deaf child's language became in all too many instances what has been called "robot language." It was not the sort of language that was normal, natural, fluent and full of meaning and pleasure as is the hearing child's language. As Dr. Davidson mentioned on several occasions, it was correct enough to satisfy the teacher, but did it satisfy the child? Does stereotyped language satisfy the deaf child of today? Does it help him to develop his personality to its highest peak, or is it dull, meaningless, useless and without pleasure to him?

It seems to me that this development came about because, in this country at that particular time, there were a number of educators who had a different concept of the language needs of the deaf child.

They apparently felt that, because of his lack of hearing, he could not acquire facility in the use of language unless it was simplified for him. As a result language was broken down bit by bit, grammatically and analytically.

These educators were sincere, conscientious and capable. I respect the motivations behind their change in techniques, but I also feel that it is necessary to examine the validity of the assumptions underlying their philosophy. Those who use the natural approach are fully aware of the difficulties the deaf child has in mastering language, but they believe that the way to make it possible for the deaf child to gain this mastery is not by altering the language itself but by making it alive and desirable for him and by seeing that it meets his needs. What psychologists tell us of the process of learning is just as applicable to the deaf child as to the hearing child.

The teacher of the deaf is, or should be, first of all a teacher. She is not a special breed, even though she must specialize in techniques for teaching the deaf. The special techniques are just a part of her work. It is the entire life of the child that she should be helping to develop. She ought to sense his needs, his longings, his strengths and his weaknesses, and find the way to meet them to the greatest satisfaction of the child himself.

Since we do not want the deaf child to be always apart from hearing children, always different in outlook, habits and attainments, we must start early to help him become one with his hearing contemporaries. For many years it has been said that the rank and file of deaf adults are too much a class by themselves and would be much better off if they were more closely attached to the population in general. If we do not wish this said of our present generation of deaf children, we shall have to see to it that they are prepared to take their place side by side with hearing people. Deafness does not have to be a social or a mental handicap! It should not be a deterrent to happy, successful living among hearing people. Nor does this mean that an ability to associate with hearing people need exclude socialization with the deaf.

Since one of the great emancipators of the deaf is the ability to use language for communication, for self-expression, for learning, for pleasure, for broadening of ideas, for socialization, for understanding of the world in which they must live, then the teaching of the language arts is probably the most crucial part of the work of the teacher of the deaf. Without the power to speak, write and comprehend the English language, no other subjects could be studied, no real participation in day-by-day living with others could take place. Actually language instruction goes on all day long. Language is the means through which all learning and growth take place. Language instruction is the path to this end and not an end in itself.

Teachers who do not believe that normal deaf children can acquire the use of language as it is used by people who can hear, lack faith in the abilities and possibilities of the deaf. There are actually many deaf children who have a better command of English than some hearing children and who can use colloquial English as well as the next person. If deaf boys and girls of average intelligence cannot use English correctly, one had better pause and consider the reason why. It could be, as was stated in one of the preceding quotations, that their early training left them without a proper concept of language and its many uses. Language was not part of them—not vital to them—not a useful tool. It lacked meaning for them. It was not something to live by! Unless the teacher *believes* that her pupils can acquire language and unless she constantly studies to improve her teaching and increase her knowledge of ways and means of teaching language, her pupils will not acquire the ability to speak, read and write good English. A teacher cannot achieve desired results by presenting exercises, drills and material of various kinds without giving any thought as to *why* she is doing so, and without questioning whether or not the results will be worthwhile. One cannot blindly follow material put out for the teaching of language to the deaf. One must study it carefully, think it through wisely, and determine for one's self what advantages can be gained from its use. Before presenting *any* material the teacher should find affirmative answers to these questions: Will this type of language work develop the child's mind, make him think for himself, reason things out, help him to associate this new information with what he already knows? Will it be useful to him over and beyond this lesson? Does it meet his needs for self-growth? Does it serve the child's purpose?

The teacher should guide her planning and her teaching so that she gives her pupils ability in the use of all the language arts which they should rightfully have. It is always more interesting to see a whole picture than just part of it! The teacher's picture of each and every child should be all inclusive—not shadowed or partly hidden by narrow thinking or the limiting outlook of someone else's prescribed suggestions or materials.

The purpose of this book, then, is to try to help teachers of the deaf reach a maximum attainment in the teaching of the language arts to the deaf, and to share with them my ideas concerning the deaf child's need for language and the ways in which my experience has taught me to meet it.

CHAPTER I

THE YOUNG CHILD
AND LANGUAGE

Perhaps of all the creations of man language
is the most astonishing.

LYTTON STRACHEY
Words and Poetry

THE HEARING CHILD

Before anyone can plunge into the teaching of language to a
deaf child he must spend considerable time in conscientious thought
and study about language—not language as it pertains to the deaf
alone but as it affects the lives of all people.

According to Webster, language is "Any means, vocal or other, of
expressing or communicating feeling or thought. The faculty of
verbal expression and the use of words in human intercourse." The
important word here is *communicating*. And what is to be com-
municated? Feelings and thoughts! One's own feelings and thoughts
as well as those of other people.

True language cannot be taught by rote. It cannot be acquired
by definition and mechanical drill. It cannot be divested of its
social significance nor removed from its social setting. To be real,
language must be fraught with meaning. There must be reasons for
using it and these reasons must spring from the individual's deep
need for making known his thoughts, ideas, needs, desires, hopes,
imaginations, joys and perplexities.

Language is a two-way affair. One must use it as we have just
stated, and must also comprehend the language of others. This
interchange makes the proper use of language a desirable accomplishment.

Any teacher of the deaf would do well to read and study some of
the books on language published for teachers of hearing children
and not especially for instructors of the deaf. The titles of a few of

these publications are listed at the back of this book. The information thus gained will provide for a deeper understanding of all problems of language teaching and foster a wider knowledge of ways and means of achieving success in the handling of this subject with the deaf.

Another very practical and delightful way of obtaining a background for teaching natural language to the deaf is to watch the hearing child's development and growth in the use of language over a period of years. To ask and to find the answers to many questions will provide the teacher with greater insight and techniques when she starts to work with the deaf. A few questions which should be answered are:

How did the baby first use words?

When did this attempt develop?

What were the first words?

In what way did one-word utterances become phrases or a collection of words?

What were the first real sentences and what was the reason for them?

What things did the child want to say?

What questions seemed most important to him?

What particular questions were asked most often?

What or who was the subject of most of the child's chatter?

What part of speech appeared most frequently and what part was used least of all?

Under what circumstances was the greatest span of conversation motivated?

The answers to these and many other questions should make the teacher of the deaf aware of the needs of her own pupils, for children are children whether they do or do not hear. There is a universal language of babyhood and childhood.

The teacher who spends time with young hearing children will discover the motivating urges to use language. The child talks because he has something to tell—or something he wants to know about—or something he wants to make different—or an idea he wants to make known—or just because he wants to be heard for companionship's sake—or sometimes because he likes the sound of his own voice. That he, at times, doesn't make much sense, doesn't in the least matter!

It is very important that the hearing child acquire much language, for the more he has the better will be his relationships with

2

his immediate family, close relatives, playmates and others with whom his lot is cast. The more language he understands and can use the more interest he finds in the postman, the bus driver, the shopkeeper and others who loom large in his small world.

Hearing children vary greatly in their use of language. Some children use only the most meager vocabulary for satisfying their immediate needs. Others go beyond this limited use of language and a new word is a delight. They frequently ask, "What does that word mean?" Such children will continually incorporate new words into their everyday speech without prodding or suggestion.

For example, one day I was walking down the street with my three-and-a-half year-old nephew and made the remark to him, "I see your shadow in the window, Peter." He replied, in a matter-of-fact voice, "That's my reflection." He liked words, he liked his words to be just right, and when he learned a new word he applied it with pleasure. A few years later I was watching Peter's four-year-old brother washing a toy. I said, "Be careful, Mike. That's breakable." He replied rather loftily, "Oh, I know. It's fragile." Words had very definite meanings to these children. Because they brought definite ideas to mind they were used frequently and correctly and with rewarding pleasure.

The growth of vocabulary on the part of young children is dependent to a large degree on the atmosphere of the home. Parents who use English well and whose vocabularies are unlimited are apt to have children whose language is excellent. This is especially true if these parents talk and read to their children a great deal.

Outside the home the teacher is the great motivating influence in the child's acquisition of language. It is she who can awaken in the child a need for facility in the use of words, a desire for greater aptitude in verbal communication, and a growing awareness of the pleasures to be found in the spoken and written word. The more socialized the child is, the more expansive his use of language. The greater his experiences, the better his vocabulary and modes of expression.

Hearing children pick up language from many sources—sometimes to the dismay of their parents! Wherever a child goes he is bombarded with language, whether it be at home, church, school, playground, park, beach or other places in city or country. Naturally, the more language he hears the more he has at his disposal. He has the tools to express himself clearly and will use them if he finds a need and if his interests are paramount.

NATURAL LANGUAGE FOR DEAF CHILDREN

Ruth Strickland, an authority on language, writes: "The spontaneity of a child's use of language is an indication of his sense of security. If he uses speech spontaneously, fluently, and clearly for his age he is growing in a satisfactory manner."[1] We may assume, then, that the young child who is maturing normally will have a good command of language. Every new experience will offer him the opportunity to continue to grow in linguistic ability.

Adults are forever intrigued by the language poured forth by their young children. They continually remark, "Where did he pick that up?" or "Where did he hear that?" Not long ago I was a guest at dinner in a home where there was a three-year-old boy who talked constantly and with surprisingly few errors. He spoke in long units of construction with the greatest of ease. He said to his father, "While you're eating your dinner, I'll try to fix this chair." Later, when we were in the car driving to my hotel, he said, "Mommy, show me the house where you lived when you were a little girl." This was real language—purposeful, social and remarkably correct. I would surmise that this child could understand many more than the six or seven thousand words generally thought to be average for a child entering first grade. The reason for this, I believe, is that he has an acute interest in what is going on about him, a deep social awareness and a desire to know and be known.

The hearing child's language grows by leaps and bounds. It is functional and imaginative. The child knows nothing of the structure of language but is motivated solely by his needs, feelings, thoughts and emotions.

"The real purpose of language," according to Mario Pei, "is to carry meaning—to transfer thought from one human brain to another. If language doesn't do this, it isn't language—it is just sound, or light, or meaningless gesture."[2] Early in life the hearing child learns that there is a purpose to language. As a baby it secures his bottle or his ball for him or it results in his being picked up. It conveys to the person caring for him what is on his mind—what he needs, likes or feels. From his earliest days he has heard words used to comfort him, amuse him, warn him or tell him about what is going on about him. Long before he can adequately handle language,

[1]Strickland, Ruth, *The Language Arts in the Elementary School.* Boston: D. C. Heath and Co., c1951, p. 59.
[2]Pei, Mario, *All About Language.* New York: J. B. Lippincott Co., c1954, p. 21.

he has an understanding of it. By the time he is able to express himself, his comprehension of language has reached great heights.

The hearing child acquires comprehensive and usable language without conscious effort or undue pressure. There is a pleasurable reward in this acquisition. The child's imitation of what he hears brings great satisfaction, not only to him but to those about him. It is amazing how quickly he travels from the simplest form of communication to actual conversation about his own thoughts, experiences and desires. The need to express one's self is paramount all through life, and the hearing child finds his way to meet this need early. Under normal conditions he develops the ability to make use of all the language necessary to his environment, and to a satisfactory adjustment at home or school and with his friends and all others with whom he comes in contact.

THE DEAF CHILD

How different is the acquisition of language on the part of the deaf child!

The deaf child differs from the hearing child only in that he cannot hear, and, not hearing, is unable to communicate in the ordinary way. His handicap is very great because of his lack of words to express his thoughts, needs and desires.

In 1955 Dr. Clarence D. O'Connor had this to say about the deaf child: "Nature imposes a heavy burden on the child who begins life with a severe hearing loss. Not only must he develop the ability to communicate without benefit of hearing but he must acquire, almost entirely through his eyes, the educational and vocational skills, knowledge and competencies so necessary for effective living. In addition, for a full life, he must build for himself a set of spiritual and moral values out of his daily experiences in a world devoid of sound, uninfluenced by the shades of meaning conveyed through audible speech. All this he must do against a backdrop of silence and in the face of public lack of sympathy for or understanding of his problem."[3]

Helen Keller has said of her deafness: "I am just as deaf as I am blind. The problems of deafness are deeper and more complex, if not more important, than those of blindness. Deafness is a much worse misfortune. For it means the loss of the most vital stimulus—

---

[3]Lexington School for the Deaf. *Eighty-eighth Annual Report,* June 30, 1955, unpaged.

the sound of the voice that brings language, sets thoughts astir, and keeps us in the intellectual company of man."[4]

No truer words were ever spoken. I have never known a blind person who would not rather have lost sight than hearing. To be blind is a serious physical handicap, but to be deaf is an intellectual handicap—a shutting out of verbal communication, either oral or written, between man and man. The handicap imposed by deafness can be overcome, but not without the acquisition of language.

Helen Keller, as we all well know, has achieved such an understanding and use of language that she has no limitations in the field of communication, either oral or written. In fact she is far superior to most hearing persons in the comprehension and use of language. She is a very exceptional person and there are many thousands of men, women and children who are aware of her life and her accomplishments.

Helen Keller is the gifted exception. Yet many deaf people have been highly successful in the various professions and fields of activity. The road may have been hard and long, but in the end these people have achieved their goals.

The young deaf child, then, starts life with a heavy handicap. He cannot learn to express himself without help. He must therefore be approached, as far as language is concerned, in a very special way. He will not, as does the hearing child, acquire language on his own. Yet he must communicate! This he does, Dr. Edna S. Levine says, by speaking "the language of behavior; the language of actions, moods and attitudes. . . . He tries his best to achieve meaningful contact with the world through his own little system of gestures and pantomime, but before very long he finds that these are not enough. He soon realizes that gestures alone cannot bring him the deeper understanding he seeks, nor make clear to others the feelings and wishes that surge within him. They provide but scant satisfaction for his curiosity, and no relief from his burden of frustration."[5] How then can the very young deaf child be made aware of the art of verbalization? The first ones to help him are his parents. Fortunate is the deaf child whose parents have early learned to accept him as a child—a child like all other children,

---

[4]Keller, Helen, *Helen Keller in Scotland*. London: Methuen & Co., 1933, p. 68.

[5]Levine, Edna S., and Groht, Mildred A., "Nursery School and the Deaf Child." *Volta Review*, 57: 5-199. (1955) p. 199-200.

a child to be loved, enjoyed, tended and helped along life's way—a child who needs understanding and especial guidance.

Parents who are adjusted to the fact that their child is deaf are in much better position to help him off to a good start in life because they will first of all treat him as any baby or child needs to be treated. They will talk to him, look at picture books with him, apply names to the things he has and the people he knows, and words to the things he does. This the parents will do in the same way in which they might converse with a hearing child—not seeking a "comeback," not trying to teach language, not forcing the child to attempt words before he is ready, not showing anxiety when he fails to respond, not being concerned about the onset of real lipreading. These parents will simply enjoy their child, play with him, help him not only to look to the face for expressions of pleasure, surprise or information, but to *like* to watch the person talking to him because the experience is a pleasurable one.

All of the foregoing should act as a basis for the later learning of language in the nursery and school. The young deaf child must first have an *understanding* vocabulary before he is taught any definite word or words. Just as a hearing child knows the meaning of words and expressions long before he tries to give back any of his own, so the deaf child must know many words and expressions before he is exposed to the teaching of specific words. His problem is not first of all speech, it is the developing of an awareness of language in human relationships. *Understanding must come before use in any instance of learning and achievement.* The little deaf child who finds satisfaction in being talked to, who is aware (sometimes with the aid of gestures or other means) of what is being talked about, will soon be found imitating his mother, father and others. Although this may not be called speech, it represents a marked advance on the road to the use of language in communication.

Not all little deaf children are started early on such a road, unfortunately. Many must wait until they reach the nursery school before they are introduced to any form of communication other than gesture or pantomime. Not long ago I asked the mother of a charming, alert, interesting and interested little boy if she talked much to him at home. She replied, "No, I don't talk to him much because he is deaf and can't hear me." Then she added, "But he often looks at me when I am talking to his brother and sister."

That same little boy learned to hold a conversation with anyone who would stop and talk to him about what he was doing in the nursery. He loved to "comment" on pictures in the books he was using. The word *comment* is quoted because of the nature of the child's attempts at speech. One had to guess what he was trying to say, principally from his accompanying facial expressions and gestures. The heartwarming aspect was that he did want to communicate and loved sharing his thoughts. We recognize that the paramount need of a young deaf child is first of all the feeling of being loved and wanted. He must feel secure in the home. He must also feel that he is a part of the family. Being talked to by his parents and others in the family group is a necessity. The talking may frequently have to be accompanied by gestures of one kind or another, but to be one of the group is a prime necessity. If the child gets the idea of what is said, that is sufficient for the time being. If he does not respond in like terms it does not matter. A hearing baby does not respond "in kind" either, yet people keep talking to him.

Dorothea McCarthy says of the hearing child, "It is quite generally agreed that the child understands gestures before he understands words, and in fact that he uses gestures himself long before he uses language proper."[6] It is my belief that a young deaf child should become acquainted with language in the same casual and informal way in which the hearing child does. It will not be in so speedy a fashion to be sure, but it will give him a good basis on which can be built a real introduction to the use and significance of language as a means of communication.

If language is ever going to be vital to the deaf child it must be attained by him, not as a lesson per se, but as a meaningful approach to a very necessary, useful and happy way of understanding himself and others. It should become second nature to him to watch the faces of people to find out what they are thinking and saying. He may take a longer time than we would wish to comprehend what is being said, to catch the key word or words which will make things clear and self-evident. With patience, however, and with the right attitude and the belief that eventually he will "catch on," success will come. He needs much more time than do his hearing contemporaries, but he is entitled to this extra time and it should be given to him ungrudgingly and unstintingly.

---

[6]McCarthy, Dorothea, "Language Development in Children," in *Manual of Child Psychology*, Carmichael, Leonard, ed. New York: John Wiley & Sons, Inc., c1946, p. 498.

With average intelligence and with no other disrupting influences, the deaf child can and will become acquainted with the meaning and use of language at a very early age. If he is to do this successfully he must be allowed to progress at his own speed and must not encounter any discouraging obstacles along the way. Overanxiety on the part of parents, too formalized attempts at teaching vocabulary, too unrealistic an approach to lipreading, and too much deadly repetition are classic examples of obstacles which can defeat a deaf child before he begins.

Home should be a happy place for the deaf child. He will not, even with the wisest parents, acquire language as he would if he could hear. Nevertheless he can be given a good start and in time he will, according to his native ability and to the kind of teaching given to him, find his way to a very satisfactory adjustment to his handicap. Deaf children of today face a far happier and more fulfilling future than those of yesteryear because so much more is known about learning, teaching and achievement in all fields of education. Today it is not uncommon for deaf children, through their ability to understand and use language, to finish high school, college or technical school and to hold their own in many professions and businesses.

CHAPTER II

THE FORMATIVE YEARS

Train up a child in the way he should go: and when he is old, he will not depart from it.

Proverbs 22:6

HAVING thought about language—what it is and what it means to the deaf child—let us now proceed to the first steps along the road to his education.

One of the big events in the child's life will be his entrance into the nursery school. Here he will find friends, both big and small. Here he will find toys and playmates, happy and wholesome activities. Most of all, he will learn the joy of communication.

A happy start is essential to the deaf child entering a nursery school. Since everything will be new, the mother should be visible and available as long as needed. This might be for a day or a week, depending upon the way in which the child adapts to his new environment. The first school days should be short, perhaps lasting only an hour or two. The child should go home for lunch, if possible, or, if a resident, go out to lunch with his mother or eat with her at school. Each child will react in his own way to the nursery. One child may cling to his mother in the beginning, while another will enter immediately into an activity or amuse himself with some toy that attracts him.

An important question to be considered in relation to the young deaf child is, "Why have a nursery school for deaf children?" If the underlying idea is to start teaching the very young deaf child formal speech, lipreading, language and reading at the early age of three or four, then the organization is not a nursery school at all. It is, rather, merely a watered down program for the teaching of the deaf and should be so labeled. The average child of nursery age is neither physiologically nor psychologically ready for formal instruction. The whole idea of a nursery school is to give to the deaf child the same start in life that his hearing brothers and sisters receive.

Therefore, a nursery in a school for the deaf should be founded upon the selfsame principles as are nursery schools for the hearing, and the people in charge should be thoroughly trained nursery school teachers—not trained teachers of the deaf, however much these folk may love little deaf children. Why should this be so? Because, at the nursery level, we need a teacher trained to concentrate on the technique of working with young children. Through observation and discussion such a teacher will develop an awareness of the proper approach to communication with the young deaf child.

An enriched nursery school program should provide children with the common experiences necessary for their physical growth and for their emotional, social and intellectual development. It should take into account the individual needs of the child. He should be accepted as he is. It is through such a program that we can build up the kind of background that will provide the basis for progress in the communication skills. Out of the hearing child's rich background of living grow his comprehension and use of language and speech. This is equally true for the deaf child.

At the Lexington School for the Deaf we believe that there is a place for tutoring in the nursery—but not for all three-year-olds. The decision about when to send the child to the tutoring room should depend to a great extent upon the child himself. We have found that some little children are ready for special work in lipreading at once, while others may not be ready for several weeks. The purpose of tutoring is to give a child individual help so that a foundation for the verbal communication of ideas may be laid.

In a book by Mary and Lawrence Frank we read: "In the preschool age the child learns gradually to communicate with others —to use language as a way of stating his questions, his needs, his demands, his feelings. Like his bodily movements, like his concepts of right and wrong, the young child's language does not evolve in orderly, precise meanings all at once."[1] These authors were not writing about deaf children but about hearing children, and yet

---

[1]Frank, Mary and Lawrence K., *How to Keep Your Child in School.* New York: Viking Press, c1950, p. 37.

11

they say the language of these children does not evolve in *orderly, precise* meanings all at once. Anyone who has had contact with hearing children must be aware of this truth. Why, then, is it so widely believed that it is necessary for the deaf child to acquire *his* language in orderly, precise meanings *all at once?* It is not a necessity!

Those in charge of a nursery school should aim to have the deaf child *want* to talk, *like* to talk and *try* to talk, and to succeed in this aim they should bear in mind the very young hearing child. How is he brought to the place where he attempts to talk? The answer is simple. Everyone talks to him—in play and for pleasure. The joy of association is felt by both the child and the speaker. What matter if, in the beginning, the conversation is entirely a one-way affair? A mother doesn't stop talking to her hearing baby because he doesn't and can't reply. She keeps on talking to him until the day when he *can* reply. She doesn't use single words in her conversation. It would not be conversation if she did, for single words do not express ideas, feelings or experiences.

The teacher must remember that though the deaf child cannot hear, he can *see.* He can sense the close companionship that accompanies the conversation of his teachers and others. He can learn at a very early age that people talk a lot—to other people as well as to him. He will associate what he sees on his teacher's face and lips with what is happening. He will make his own deductions—perhaps not the first nor the second or even the fifty-second time, but eventually!

Lipreading should start at once in the nursery as in the home. It's never too soon, for lipreading is language. In all lipreading the emphasis should be placed not so much on the words as on the *ideas.* Lipreading in the nursery, as elsewhere, is not a *subject* to be learned. It is never to be used as a classroom trick at certain periods of the day. It is not something for which a child receives a star when he does respond and a frown when he does not. As Van Riper says: "The word should be presented and evoked only in the appropriate context. It should never be used for display alone. It should be useful to the child in controlling his environment. Attempts to teach or produce these words should only be carried out when the child is attentive, happy and responsive."[2] The habit of giving commands such as *run, jump, fall* or *bow* is pernicious, to my way

---

[2]Van Riper, C., *Teaching Your Child to Talk.* New York: Harper & Brothers, c1950, p. 58.

of thinking. Why even bother to teach a verb like *bow?* Who goes around bowing these days? A time will come when that verb will appear in reading but the nursery or preschool is no place to make its acquaintance. To command a child to run around the room is a poor way to acquaint him with the verb *run.* He isn't allowed to run around the room except during that particular lipreading period. And why should Mary be told to shut the door, and then told to open it? These commands do not give a very comprehensive use of the verbs *open* and *shut.* And of what interest are these commands to little children? None!

No doubt the idea behind the use of action work in the learning of verbs was to attain repetition in lipreading. But this was not conceptual language teaching. Teachers using action work probably hold the idea that since young children enjoy being active, this type of exercise is based on the children's interests. However, if one examines lessons based on action work, it soon becomes apparent that the purpose they serve is that of the teacher and not of the pupils. Let us take as an example the child who is told to skip and thereupon vigorously begins skipping around the room. His enthusiasm is soon curbed because the teacher doesn't really want him to tear around the room; she merely wants to determine whether or not he can lipread the word *skip.* There are so many normal ways to teach a child the language he needs. The best way by far is to make use of the words, be they verbs, nouns or any other part of speech, in natural situations. The teacher must make use of every possible situation or experience, all day long, day in and day out. Her remarks might run like these, used when required, "Don't run, walk." In the yard she might say: "Run after Tommy." "Let's catch Mary." "Run fast." "Let's see who can run the fastest!" There will be endless occasions when the verb *run* is in order.

Let us take as one more example the verbs *open* and *shut.* These are useful verbs to a little child, but they will not be very usable if he becomes acquainted with them by opening and shutting doors. Possible uses might be: "It's warm in here. Let's open the window."—"What do you think is in this box? Why don't you open it?" Over and over again these verbs can be used in talking to the children when necessity calls for them—*meaningful repetition is what counts.* A wise teacher will find ways and means of getting this very necessary repetition. A child understands language when it is given to him where circumstances help him interpret its meaning—when it is related to what he is doing or thinking.

NATURAL LANGUAGE FOR DEAF CHILDREN

It is imperative that the deaf child be given a firm foundation on which to build his ever growing need for language. This foundation should be laid in the nursery by those who are responsible for the child's growth in living, learning, understanding and using language. Many deaf pupils lack a broad and intelligent use of language because they were introduced to the idea of language by being taught single words out of context—words that merely named an object or an act but conveyed no feeling or idea—words that required no thought or provided no new experience.

Learning to think, feel and express himself through the use of language is a prime requisite for the nursery child. He is as anxious to communicate with all those about him as is the little hearing child who chatters all day long. Therefore, from the beginning, his introduction to language should be very rewarding to him. No young nursery child, or any age deaf child for that matter, should be introduced to language by means of formal, stereotyped, stilted, repetitious exercises. Exercises do not constitute language, but conversations do.

In conversing happily with the nursery child, many words will stand out and become familiar to him. He soon will recognize such words as *home, mommy* and *daddy,* not only in lipreading but through the hearing aid if he has sufficient residual hearing to allow this. These words are of vital import to him. By means of family photographs he will associate the words with his recall of people and things at home. He does not need a prepared list of family names, for instance, for his family is an individual group, the same as every other child's. I remember seeing a three-year-old look wide-eyed at her tutor's new dress. In attempted speech the youngster said, "Mommy, same, home." The teacher replied, "What! Mommy has a dress like mine?" The child nodded and reiterated, "Same, same," and the teacher said, "The same kind of dress. Well, well! Do you like it? Does Mommy like hers?" I give this incident as an example of communication between teacher and child. Later, when the child went out into the big playroom, she was observed trying to tell another child about the coincidence of the identical dresses.

I do not think it wise, in fact I almost think it presumptuous, for anyone to give a teacher a list of words to follow in teaching her young pupils. Each child should develop his own vocabulary. There may be many similar words on these individual lists but they will have evolved from different circumstances. The teacher must be on the alert for conditions and situations which will afford the right approach to the teaching of new vocabulary. Take the word *sweater,* as an example. For little Mary it might develop in this manner, as she appears in the tutoring room in a torn sweater. Teacher shows surprise and concern and says, "What happened to your *sweater?*" By means of gestures and dramatics, it becomes clear that Mary caught her sweater on the chain of the swing and tore it. The conversation continues, "We'll ask Mommy to get another *sweater,* a nice clean one. Maybe tonight Mommy will fix this *sweater.*" When a fresh sweater is produced the conversation may run like this, "Oh, here's a nice, clean, white *sweater.*" Mary volunteers, through gesture and an approach to speech, that Mommy washed this sweater at home. The tutor puts this information into language: "Mommy washed this *sweater* when you were home. That's why it's nice and clean. This *sweater* isn't torn, either. Let's put this one on now. You look sweet in this *sweater.*" Mary acknowledges the look of admiration and nods her head in approval. To be sure Mary does not yet know the word *sweater* very well, but she will in time. The teacher must keep the word in mind and find further uses for it. For example, she can change a doll's sweater, or talk about some other child's sweater, or find pictures of little boys and girls who are wearing sweaters, or fold a sweater to fit into a suitcase, and so on.

Not so might Janie be introduced to this word. Her introduction might come on her birthday when she comes to the nursery proudly displaying a new and fancy sweater. Here the conversation might obviously run something like this: "Janie, that's a beautiful *sweater.* I think your mommy sent it to you. It's a lovely *sweater,* and look at the flowers on it. Later we'll have a party in the yard and you can wear your pretty *sweater* and everyone will tell you how nice you look in your new *sweater!*" Janie can readily gather from her teacher's expression that her sweater is an especially nice one and is being admired. Janie doesn't yet know the word *sweater* either, but like Mary, she will in time. During the weeks that follow she is apt to lose a sweater, forget her sweater, have clean or soiled sweaters, get paint on a sweater, change sweaters with another child or maybe fall heir to a new sweater for her favorite doll. Given time, experience and repetition, Janie and all her nursery playmates will learn to lipread remarks about sweaters.

How different the above type of teaching is from the old and uninteresting way of pasting a picture of a sweater on a chart with pictures of other articles of dress and saying to a child, "Show me the sweater," or "Show me the coat." That method of getting repetition had no real value for a child. It did nothing to build up his concept of words as a means of communication. The examples of the manner in which Mary and Janie acquired a vocabulary are cited to show that a nursery child's vocabulary can grow individually, meaningfully and pleasurably. We need to give meanings to our words if they are to become useful to the child, and he should and will absorb these meanings through use.

Lipreading is of inestimable value to the deaf child. It is the foundation for all learning of language. The deaf boy or girl who is a good lipreader will understand what language is—will sense its value in all his associations with others. He will take for granted the fact that talking (or communication) is what makes for pleasant relationships with other people—for understanding, expression, friendliness and happiness.

It is in the nursery that the first steps toward making a good lipreader are taken. The child who has the benefit of a nursery program has a decided advantage over the one who has not. It will make all the difference in the world to the child who gets a good beginning, who learns to read the lips in an easy, relaxed manner, who unconsciously feels that watching a person talk will help him learn things, do things, have a happy time, feel secure, loved and wanted. He should read not just lips, but facial expressions, mannerisms, personality and general characteristics of the person who is talking to him. He should learn to watch the face for expressions of pleasure, hope, displeasure, assistance and anticipation. He must see the same words emphasized often, and first of all these should be usable words—not merely nouns and verbs, but other parts of speech. For example the teacher might say: "These are *your* rubbers. Please put them away." "Get *your* coat. Not Jerry's—*yours*." "That's a picture of *your* home." "You don't need *your* sweater today. It's warm." "*Your* coat is dirty. Let's brush it." It is amazing to those who work with very young deaf children to see how many expressions they pick up on their own.

When the Lexington School started its nursery there were several children enrolled who were under three years of age. One day an incident occurred which showed us clearly that constant repetition under meaningful conditions would give these babies an insight into usable words. Each day the nursery teacher would wave good-bye to the children and say "Bye-bye." This was a natural thing to do and we thought little about it. But one morning Miss Mary New, former assistant principal at Lexington, took one of the babies to demonstrate the technique of talking to the child and of emphasizing key words to let the child see, feel and hear how they sounded. When she had finished and wished the child to return to the nursery, she said, "Go along now. Bye-bye." The little one went off but shortly was back with her hat and coat. Saying "Bye-bye" every day when she left for home had taken root even though she had yet to learn that the phrase could be used in a different sense. Little children of nursery age, with a right attitude toward lipreading, will accept as a normal thing the watching of a speaker's face and expression.

Lipreading is an art and fortunate the deaf child who early masters that art—who learns to catch an idea or a key word and get the gist of what is being said to him, even though he cannot repeat word for word what the speaker has said. Why should he? Those of us who hear cannot repeat word for word the things that are spoken to us. We listen for *content,* not for separate words. So should the deaf watch for clues that will reveal the content of a communication.

As I have already indicated, all young children are not ready for special tutoring (lipreading, imitative speech and work with the hearing aid) at the same time. No pressure should be brought upon any of the children. *Learning* goes on all day whether the children are going into the tutoring room for individual attention or are out in the nursery playroom or yard. First of all they need to develop as normal children do. It takes time for very young children to want to participate in a group—to learn lessons in social relationships—to learn to do things for themselves—to develop an imagination. These are important aspects of nursery training. Little deaf children, like all children, love to dress up and pretend. A costume box filled with assorted old pocketbooks, scarves, hats, skirts, shoes and the like, will provide endless ways for the children to give vent to their imaginations. When they dicover these treasures they will soon be pretending to be a mother pushing her baby in a carriage, or going shopping, or taking a walk with daddy and the children, or strolling along carrying a parasol, or playing house or having a tea party. Any or all of these activities give the teacher wonderful opportunities to evoke conversation— "Well, you're going to the store." "That's a lovely pocketbook." "Your baby looks very pretty." "Are you a mother (or a daddy)?"

17

Building a house, bridge or roadway with large blocks also brings forth communication and opportunities for casual lipreading. In fact there can be an unending use of language in the nursery area—stories, books, milk and cookie periods, lunch and nap periods, normal child activities and incidental occurrences such as spilling milk or upsetting paint—all these and many other day-by-day happenings provide opportunities for the use of language. Children will learn of their own accord to lipread such repetitive remarks as: "Wash your hands." "It's time for lunch." "Get the cookies." "Johnny, it's your turn to pass the cookies today." "Hang up your coat." "Put on your boots."

At the Lexington School, where there are two distinct nurseries, the children move from Nursery I (two-and-a-half or three years at entrance) to Nursery II (four years at entrance).

The program in Nursery II is not unlike that of the beginning nursery except that the children, having had previous training, understand much more language, can spend a little more time with the tutors, can in many cases work in pairs and can give back many speech sounds through imitation and touch. I hasten to add, however, that formal development of the speech sounds is not practiced here. If a child can give a good k in a word he is trying to say, well and good, but the teacher does not struggle to perfect any sound the child is not ready to give.

Many trips are taken by the children and discussed with them. They go out to buy, to look, to see, to play, to find new experiences. Longer stories are told. Books suitable to any four-year-olds are looked at and read. The children go to the school library to exchange books. In the visual aid room they see short movies or stills especially suited to their age. These are talked about by the tutors both before and after the showing. (Movies should not be more than 8 or 10 minutes in length.) The children in Nursery II go to eurythmics, as do the children in Nursery I, but being a year older their program is geared to their needs and inclinations. They go to art class in addition to the painting and clay modeling that they do in the nursery area. Their vocabulary is increased and each child has his own book in which he pastes pictures of things he has, likes or knows about.

The four-year-olds do not learn to read or write. Like many hearing children their age they recognize their names and some of them recognize a few other words "on their own." They are still being saturated with the use and meaning of oral language and constantly attempt to communicate not only with the adults but with the other children.

They have learned to recognize some printed words, not because they have been taught to read but because they were exposed to them quite casually in simple charts the teachers have made in connection with nursery activities. For example, at this age they learn to recognize their own and the other children's names by seeing them repeatedly on the "cubbies" where the children hang their clothing; on their art work; or on a chart showing a picture of a child with a tray of cookies. Under the picture is a slot into which is inserted the name of the child whose turn it is to pass the tray.

There are many other ways in which the nursery teachers build reading and number readiness. In our Nursery II, the teacher has a very colorful attendance chart which the children love. There is a picture of each child and adult in the nursery. Every morning, as they check the attendance, each child who is there uncovers the flap over his picture. They then count the number of girls and boys who are present. The children quite unconsciously learn to count as well as to recognize the printed names. Again, our children learn to understand that the printed word conveys meaning, even though they can't decipher its exact meaning, by seeing the nursery teacher hang a sign on the door every time they leave for the playground. Pretty soon the children are reminding the teacher to put up the sign before they go out. This is true reading readiness.

Again there is no definite list of words to be lipread. Each child has his own vocabulary. In most instances there are many of the same words and expressions in these vocabularies. The children are naturally interested in many similar activities and experiences and have common possessions, thoughts and ideas. These individual vocabularies grow as the children grow and their activities widen.

The important thing to remember is that a nursery, whether for three or for four-year-olds, is not a classroom and should not be run like one. It *is* a place for playing, learning, growing in awareness of language and its uses, becoming socialized and receiving both love and understanding. The nursery is an important part of any school and requires the best to be had in equipment, personnel and supervision.

CHAPTER III

GROWING IN AWARENESS

A little work, a little play,
To keep us going—and so, good-day!
A little warmth, a little light,
Of love's bestowing—and so, good-night!

GEORGE DU MAURIER
Trilby

THE preschool should be a place of preparation where the five-year-old deaf child, who has had nursery training, can receive the background he must have before he enters the first grade. This is where he must be fortified with a genuine understanding of language—what it means and what it does. What he accomplishes here will have a vital influence on the rest of his school life and even beyond it. The responsibility of the preschool teacher is therefore very great. She must know what real *teaching* is and she must be imaginative and original as well as knowledgeable. She must be aware of the needs of all five-year-olds and particularly of the deaf child. She must know where he is going and what he will need to know when he gets there.

Before going into specific details about what should be accomplished in the preschool it might be well to review a little of what has been said and written about learning in general and learning to use language in particular. We have been told that learning can be achieved only by appropriate activity. I should put the accent on the word *appropriate*. Keeping this in mind the teacher will not suggest that a child put a flower *under* the table as a way of using that preposition, or say to him, "Put your handkerchief under your chair." She should remember that we must all learn a thing in the way in which it will be used, and she must see that there is the right motivation present for real learning on the part of her pupils.

The teacher herself must be flexible and able to make use of more flexible teaching methods. In addition to all this she must be able to guide her charges effectively. Does this mean that she must be superhuman? I think not! A teacher who loves and understands children, who is conscientious, who is well prepared, and who earnestly desires to guide her pupils in the proper paths of learning will measure up to the highest qualifications. Certainly teachers of the deaf are not lacking in dedication.

There are certain truths about the acquisition of language by all children that the teacher of the deaf ought to bear in mind. In the book, *The Development of Learning in Young Children*, we read, "Understanding of the significance of words and phrases may be acquired before capacity to pronounce or to make use of the words in voluntary speech."[1] This, it seems to me, lends weight to the method of using a great deal of lipreading and some silent reading before working on the development of speech sounds and writing and reading. In the same book the author also says, "It must always be borne in mind that the capacity for using language is developed through practice."[2] If the hearing child needs practice in learning to use language, the deaf child's need is much greater and he needs this practice in the same natural, normal way. This knowledge should make the teacher wary of going too fast in giving new language and of adding too many new language principles before the children have had sufficient practice to become familiar with those already presented.

Language should be taught to the child in such a way that through its use he can express those things he thinks and feels. Through his use of language he will reveal the extent to which he is growing mentally and emotionally, and to which he is changing from an *I* to a *we* approach to daily living.

The deaf child should develop his own language and do so from his own needs, feelings and experiences.

The teacher of young deaf children should know *what* language to teach as well as *how* and *when* to teach it. Above all she should understand the *why* of all her work. The *why* of teaching

---

[1]Wagoner, Lovisa C., *The Development of Learning in Young Children*. New York: McGraw-Hill Book Co., c1933, p. 184.

[2]*Ibid.*, p. 187.

language should be settled first. Is a certain language principle, for example, being taught at a given time because someone says it must be presented to the child at that particular time, or is it being taught because the children have indicated a very definite need for it? It is the latter question that should be answered in the affirmative.

Next comes the *what* to teach. The language taught to the child should answer his needs, develop in him the desire to express his thoughts and feelings and give to him the tools to do so clearly and correctly. The answer to *when* to teach a given language usage should be: When circumstances or conditions will make clear to the child the meaning of the language in question so that he can make his own interpretation of it and sense his own need of it.

Now comes the question of *how* to teach new language—a question that bothers many a teacher. The answer is that this should be done *in a natural way,* making full use of the child's experiences, interests and needs. It should never be done through the use of extraneous materials, drill sentences or artificial exercises devoid of personal interest and entirely outside the child's need for the language being taught.

Every teacher should bear in mind, before attempting to teach language at any level, that if language is to be spontaneous it must be fully understood and must come forth from a pleasant attitude of mind. It is not enough for a teacher to know the mechanics of grammar or have skill in using all language principles and constructions. She must develop a *spirit* about it—make her pupils eager to talk or write—make it second nature to put thoughts into *words.* Ease and freedom of thought bring out natural expression. The child who is disgruntled, fussy, jealous or quarrelsome will never do interesting work—nor will the child who thinks language is a difficult subject.

The teacher who finds herself with a class that has been brought up in a very formal manner will gradually have to develop a spirit of ease and friendliness. This may take time and ingenuity, but it can be done, if the pupils are not expected to burst forth into a joyous attitude all at once. Barriers can be removed by friendly contact and a child can be won over in friendship and made to work with his teacher and his classmates in happy cooperation.

To obtain natural expression from a deaf child there must be a spirit as well as an ability in the use of language. Sometimes deaf children perform far below their ability because they have not received sufficient encouragement or help. One can't help a child too much if the help is guidance!

Having thought about the importance and need of the ability to use and comprehend language, let us go back to some of the fundamentals of the program in a preschool class of deaf children between five and six years of age. The emphasis here should be on oral communication through speech, lipreading and prereading skills and, to a minor extent, on prewriting skills. The use of simple, everyday expressions should not only be encouraged but insisted upon when a need for them is indicated. The value and necessity of language should be continually stressed so that the children will always think in terms of language and attempt to express themselves verbally.

The big difference between the nurseries and the preschool is that the five-year-old child can take more direct teaching, can sit in a small group for short periods of time, can and should participate in what is being discussed, and attempt to use language in larger units of expression.

The ideal number of pupils in a preschool class would be six or seven. Since this situation is rarely attainable, a teacher can handle eight if she plans wisely. No more than that should be considered if real achievement is to be gained.

The preschool classroom should not be set up as a formal schoolroom. In addition to the individual tables and chairs, the room should have a play area which would include such things as dolls, bed, table, dishes, ironing board, toy cupboard, stove, blocks, cars, boats and other toys. There should be a table and bookcase in the reading corner.

The emphasis should still be on lipreading which clarifies and broadens the child's concept of words, phrases and sentences. Every teacher of the deaf knows that it is possible for a deaf child to learn to recognize words from the lips and yet not acquire an understanding of the language as hearing people understand it. It may be only a trick of the memory, with no mental growth at all. In such cases the children do not get an understanding of the significance of words in communicating thought. If a deaf child is to grow in language he must thoroughly understand it. Little children who are accustomed to being talked to will, by the time they are five and in a preschool class, be able to think things through by means of language. Sensing what the end of a story is going to be, figuring out situational clues suggested through pictures or imaginative play, should all reveal a growing awareness of the meaning of words in communication and thinking.

A child between five and six should think of his experiences in terms of language and should be able, with help from the teacher, to tell the rest of the class what he did that was fun, or what he saw, or found or bought. If this information is fresh and interesting it should be written on the blackboard by the teacher (using manuscript writing) so that the children can see it written as well as spoken. The blackboard should be used first, but later on the information could be written on newsprint. The rest of the class will recognize names and, as time goes on, many other words. Eventually the whole sentence will be understood. The children will be reading what they already know. So-called "class news" is easily read by preschool pupils, for they have first had the experiences and understand the situations.

There should be no drill on this written news. That is not the purpose of it. It should be written as it is discussed and should reinforce what has been said. Illustrations can be used at first to clarify a word, but later, when the children can recognize a word, the illustration can be eliminated. If Susie wishes to tell the class about her new red sandals, the teacher might write—"Susie's mother bought her some new red sandals yesterday."—and follow this with a drawing in red chalk of a pair of sandals like Susie's new ones. Or if Bobby has a Bandaid on his knee, this can be written up and followed by a picture of Bobby with a Bandaid on his knee. The teacher need not write about each child every day, but should make sure that all children are represented during the week.

Only new and special things should be written and the news should not contain such dull and routine items as calendar and weather data. A rain that prevents a trip might be news, as might be the first snow storm, but weather is not ordinarily vital to a five-year-old. The children should find the date on the calendar (preferably a large one) and the day and date should be written at the top of the news article.

This sharing of happenings is a very important part of the language preparatory work in the preschool, or any other grade for that matter. This phase of the daily program should not be conducted in a routine fashion as a lesson that must be covered, but rather as a sharing of thoughts in which all are interested. There

③

Some children brought a white cat to see us.

Vickie gave it water.

We held it.

We liked it.

Next week we will go up ↑ to the hospital for an eye test.

Janice is sick. We're sorry.
Johnny is sick. We're sorry
Hurry up - Get better - Come to school.

Five-year-olds have many interests.

might conceivably be a day when no news is written on the blackboard at all because nothing of note has transpired or because the children are excited about some forthcoming activity or plan. Generally speaking, little children desire earnestly to talk about things that are of importance to themselves.

There are many necessary expressions which should be learned by preschool children and used when required. Five-year-olds at our school use many such expressions. If a child is talking to the class and someone is not looking the child will automatically say, "Watch me," or "Look at me." Other expressions needed and used by preschool children might well be: "Please move." "I can't see." "May I be first?" "May I come next?" "Stop that." "Don't bother me." "Don't be silly." "I have some." "I'm through." "I know that." "Let me see." "It's time for lunch." "Wait for me." "What's that?" "That's awful." "Please show me." "It's my turn." "What's that for?" "Why?"

Expressions should only be taught when called for, and never in a drill. The number the children will use will depend upon their needs. The teacher should insist, however, that a child use them when the need is present. If he indicates that he can't see a picture, for example, he should be told to say, "I can't see." If this is done day in and day out, the deaf child will eventually use the expression of his own accord both inside and outside the classroom. It will become a part of him, and the more natural expressions he knows the more habitual will his use of language become. Let me add here that these expressions should not be used as a speech lesson. The child in the preschool may at first only give an approximation of the speech of the remarks, but in due time he will be able to speak more clearly and correctly. The emphasis at the moment should be on the development and use of language as a means of communication, and an awareness of the value of language in terms of satisfactory living.

I cannot stress lipreading too much, for in the nurseries and preschool it is of greatest importance. I refer to casual or general lipreading—not so-called exact lipreading, where a child must give back word for word what has been said. The following statement, appearing in *Guiding the Young Child,* seems appropriate: "The teacher must be conscious of children's understanding or lack of understanding of words and phrases they use. She cannot take it for granted that a word spoken is a word understood."[3] Though the foregoing was written for the teacher of the hearing, what wonderful advice for a teacher of the deaf! In the same book we read, "She (the teacher) should translate the experience into words at the time (of its happening.)"[4] For the deaf child this can be done in what we call casual lipreading and, on occasion, in the "news" written by the teacher.

---

[3]Heffernan, Helen, ed., *Guiding the Young Child.* Boston: D. C. Heath and Co., c1951, p. 102.

[4]*Ibid.*

Everyone helps.   Photo by Norman Crane

More than anything else in the first few years, lipreading should be conversation—conversation about everything that touches the child—his home, his family, his friends, his school, his toys, his activities, his childhood joys and sorrows. These conversations should be natural and spontaneous. The teacher should make it easy for the child and *expect* him to understand. She should be patient, but this does not mean maintaining a pained forbearance. There should be laughter, fun, contentment and genuine happiness in the classroom. Never think that the movement of lips is all there is to lipreading.

Normal deaf children who are good lipreaders usually have good oral and written language and are good readers. Their contacts with the hearing are satisfactory, normal and pleasant. Deaf children who have a true concept of language will want to use language and will not be satisfied with a one-way affair in communication. They will want to take part in conversations at home or in school. They will have something to say and will wish to say it.

When the young child has this desire to talk and also has the language to clothe his thoughts, what about his speech? That is a problem which is almost insurmountable for the teacher who expects correct speech at all times from young pupils. The child's chattering will not be an example of correct pronunciation, because his language ability at five or six will far outdistance his progress

27

in speech at this level. This is bound to be true as it is true with hearing children. But should we limit what the deaf child has to say because he hasn't mastered all the sounds that are involved in the words he wants to say? I would say emphatically, "No! Let him express himself."

Many years ago at Lexington School, when we first started to have our five-year-olds ask questions and talk about all sorts of things, the speech was pretty much of a jumble. The children had *so* much to say and lacked a corresponding ability in speech. Would this discrepancy ever be overcome? We hoped and we trusted. We believed that it was worth a trial, so we stood fast in our belief that the first step was to give the child the right concepts of the language he needed, make him *want* to talk, *love* to talk, have a lot to talk about, expect to be talked to and expect to be understood. We wanted the habit of communication to be firmly established. Of what use is perfect speech if a child has nothing to say—or if the perfect speech is used only in unrelated, uninteresting or teacher-made sentences? Of what use is speech if the child cannot use it in the same way and for the same reason the hearing child uses it? He must have speech and it should be good speech, intelligible to others. First, however, the deaf child needs time to acquire an understanding of language.

So in our natural language program we ventured! We poured in language concepts. We used every opportunity possible to give the children "a language sense." We had no set vocabulary—each child developed his own. What sort of vocabularies were they? They contained the names of people they knew, things they used in and out of school, places that were familiar—good words, important words, silly words, *children's* words. We helped them to say what they wanted to say, regardless of what language principle was involved. There was no difficulty here. Deaf children of this age have no need for difficult grammatical forms, nor do hearing children. They learned countless remarks such as: "We're early." "Martha's late." We used any and every *needed* verb form. In short, we used the language demanded by the occasion. The children *led* and did not follow blindly. Would their language be mixed up later? We believed not and our faith was justified.

Can all deaf children be taught this way? I feel certain that all deaf children of normal intelligence and normal emotional balance can be taught in this way, and that they will be happier, more natural, more normal in behavior and more communicative.

Not all children, whether hearing or deaf, progress at the same rate of speed. One child will take two years to do what another child can do in one year. How fast the deaf child moves along depends upon many things—among them, his early home influences and training, his attitude toward grown-ups, his emotional stability, his feeling of security, his intelligence, his use of his own particular resources, his natural gift or aptitude for lipreading. It is very important to remember that the point to be considered is not how fast he progresses, but how well.

How about the slow learner? Will he profit by this approach? I would say that he will accomplish more by this approach than he will in a barren, stereotyped and artificial manner of teaching. He may be a slow learner and a slow thinker, but he is still a little child and must be reached as one. It seems to me that just because he *is* slow, the approach to him should be easy and natural and should allow for a great deal of meaningful repetition and review.

All five-year-old children are full of questions. They like to know all about many things. They like to guess about things, too. The children in a preschool class should learn questions, *not* question forms. There is a vast difference between the two! There are questions children want to ask often and these should be taught as expressions—"May I see it?" "What's in the box?" "Where's Mary?" "Where are we going?" "Who's that?" "What's the matter?" "How many are there?" "Are they for everybody?" "May we play with them now?" These are only a few. At first the children will need a great deal of help from the teacher each time a question is asked, but by the end of the year many questions will be used frequently and with less help.

It is amazing how much general information can be gained by preschool pupils in playing a guessing game about something wrapped up. Our children love to surprise their classmates by bringing various articles to school and making everyone guess what is in the package or box. In the beginning a child may say only the word *red*. The teacher helps him to say, "Is it red?" and writes the question on the blackboard. If the owner replies that it is not red, some other child may ask, again with help from the teacher, "Is it blue?" Later the question, "What color is it?" comes to the fore. The children like to feel the package. Little by little this curiosity will bring forth such questions as, "Is it made of wood, or of plastic, or of iron, or of tin?" Some five-year-olds know the names of many materials. They bring in things made of ivory, for instance, and demand the name of that material. Other questions preschool children learn to ask by the end of the year are: "How many things have you?" "Are they pretty?" "Where did you get them?" "Who gave them to you?" "Did you buy them?" "Is it heavy?" "Is it something to eat?" There should be no set order for asking these questions and the same question should not be asked more than once. If Betty has asked, "Is it something to eat?" and the question has been answered in the affirmative, the teacher should not allow Billy to ask, "Is it something to play with?" She should explain the importance of watching and say that Betty had answered that it was something to *eat* and that we do not play with food. If Patty asks, "Is it round?" and is told that it is, then further questions about shape should not be asked during the game. This is a *guessing* game and not a question form drill. There must be thought and meaning behind the questions. Children quickly learn that if a thing is meant to be worn they obviously cannot ask if it is something to play with or to eat. While the apparent emphasis is on the fun of guessing, every opportunity should be taken to make clear to the children the reason, value and use of each and every question. The teacher should help a child who is having difficulty expressing his question.

The use of pictures in the preschool class can be most profitable in many aspects of the day-by-day program. Much lipreading can be accomplished by talking about the various people or things in a picture, or stories suggested by the picture can be told to the children. Pictures provide countless opportunities for making deductions as to circumstances, finding situational clues, making inferences as to the feelings and conversation of the characters depicted, guessing what might have preceded the action that is portrayed, and anticipating what might follow. This is of inestimable value in training a child to think things through and in increasing his verbal concepts. I remember observing several five-year-olds who were looking at a picture of a family in a living room, all gathered around a large crate which had evidently just been opened. The faces showed surprise or joy or excitement and all looked very happy. The teacher asked the children why they thought all members of the family were smiling and happy—why the children were excited—why one little boy was tugging at his daddy and obviously wanting him to hurry and get "the thing" out of the crate. Three of the children deduced that the whole family was happy because daddy had bought a new T.V. set. Two of the children needed help to see the situation. One child wanted to tell about a T.V. set her family got for Christmas.

Pictures used for developing the ability to see situations should be such as would interest any children of five years of age—and in the beginning the situations should be rather obvious. As time goes on the conditions in the picture could be less evident and allow for more inferences. This type of work provides an excellent background for the teaching of conceptual language and for its use in everyday affairs. A lesson of this sort should not be formalized and should not be forced. The pictures themselves, plus the teacher's manner and her manifestations of interest, should give the right motivation for the children to want to gather in a circle and look at the pictures and have the teacher talk about them.

As a background for reading, children should be introduced to a series of pictures showing several steps of an experience. The teacher should at first talk to the class about what is happening in the pictures and she should show each phase of the story in sequence. Such sets of pictures may be found in many prereading workbooks. The pictures can be cut out and pasted on oak tag strips for longer wear and easier handling. After the children have had much experience in talking about such stories, they should have many opportunities to take a set of pictures and arrange them in order. Such activities are of great value in helping children to visualize conditions or events in the order of their occurrence and to reason out these experiences.

Pictures for this kind of interpretation can be found on the covers of the *Saturday Evening Post*. These are generally high in interest value—imaginative, appealing and often humorous. With a little ingenuity, a teacher can convert these covers (which are usually one-frame pictures) into sequence stories by folding back or otherwise covering up key parts of the picture. For example, with a cover showing many children in a pediatrician's waiting room, interest was considerably heightened in one class by the simple expedient of covering up that part of the picture showing the doctor emerging from his office to admit the next child—the only child in the room who was looking frightened.

Another basis for reading can be found in various directions for "duties" in the classroom. Having a chart with slots for inserting a child's name and his duty for the day, or using charts to show where the class has gone, help the children to recognize language that is functional and in constant use. For example, one chart in our school is made of oak tag and consists of two sheets held together in the center by a brass paper fastener. On the bottom sheet are pictures indicating various activities. The top sheet has a piece cut out and this sheet can be moved around to show where the children have gone. A child fixes the chart to the proper place and hangs it on the outside of the schoolroom door. After returning to the room the sign is removed and another is put up stating, "We are in our room."

There must be many opportunities for language growth in the preschool as well as in the primary or lower school. Deaf children should not be limited in the development of language because of the limiting approach to the teaching of it on the part of their teachers. It requires a resourceful, imaginative and creative teacher to maintain a classroom atmosphere that is conducive to proper learning. The teacher should make the using of language so much a part of herself and the children in her class that they will accept language as naturally as will a hearing child. They should consider it a vital necessity to communication and to happy and interesting contacts with other children and adults.

The teacher must constantly bear in mind the need for repetition of the language she wishes to teach. Through conversation, news, storytelling, expressions and questions the child can acquire number concepts, identification of colors, idiomatic language and general information that most five-year-olds pick up. I believe children should learn to recognize colors through conversation and news items about their toys, clothing, and other possessions, and through picture book and magazine illustrations. Little children love matching the colors in their clothing to identical colors in other things. Hearing children learn to know the colors as they are exposed to them, and as they have a desire to know the color of various belongings and other objects. They do not need a color chart to learn to reel off the names of the color samples on it.

Number concepts are gained more rapidly when they are developed concretely and used with things the children have, use or know about. The lipreading of numbers should be done in connection with language—should appear in news items (Bobby brought three cars to school this morning), in questions (Vicky, will you get me two pieces of chalk?), and in casual lipreading (Yesterday I saw a mother bird and two tiny little birds outside on the fire escape.) Will the preschool children get each and every word? Not yet—but they will get the concept of a large bird and two small

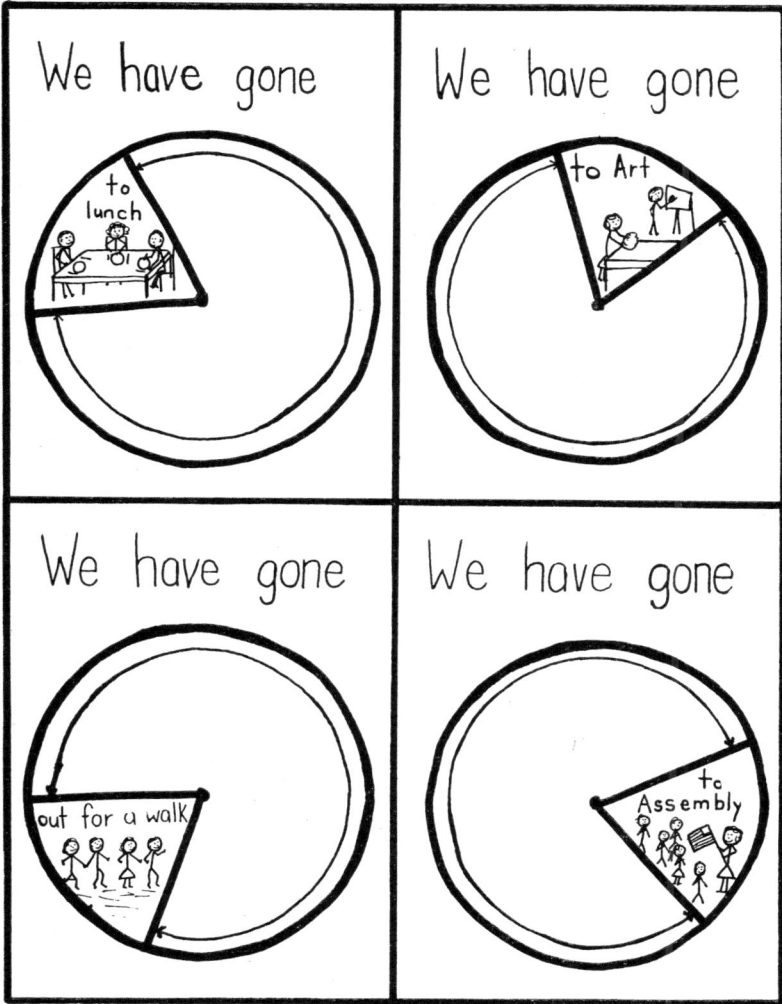

We have gone to lunch

We have gone to Art

We have gone out for a walk

We have gone to Assembly

Functional reading. See page 32.

ones. Children love to count and should have the experience of counting sufficient cookies, crayons or papers so that there will be one for each child. Counting toys and objects to see if there are enough to go around is meaningful to any child.

Through day-by-day communication much language is acquired incidentally. The program should be flexible. It should by all means allow for as many modes of transportation and to as many places as possible. The children might go to the firehouse, the postoffice, or to the store to buy something for the classroom, to purchase a present for someone who is having a birthday, or to get the ingredients for making Jello or cocoa. These are but a few of the many activities that take place outside the classroom and which add much in the way of language for everyday occurrences. Whenever feasible children should go to the teacher's home and see where she lives and what she does in her home. They should learn that a teacher is a real person, for this knowledge will bring about a closer feeling between pupil and teacher.

Exposing the deaf child to communication is the all-governing aim of the preschool teacher, for through the use of language the deaf child, like his hearing brother, matures normally and happily. The teacher must remember that the deaf child must be given many opportunities for using language, while the hearing child will more often than not find his own.

Deaf children need a skillful teacher—one who can saturate them with language and supply their need for it. At the same time the teacher must know where she is going and arrive there on a straight and clear path. She should know how much allowance to make for each child and also how much she can require in the way of adequate return. She should repeat very often, *in natural circumstances,* the language she desires the child to learn.

The teacher who demands perfection from a preschool child is not only going to be badly disappointed but she is going to be a great drawback to the child. It would be far better if she could remember and accept the fact that a hearing child, in his early attempts at using language, is allowed to make errors—to misuse, leave out or mispronounce words. One wonders how it ever came about that the deaf child, when first attempting to use language, was expected to use perfect grammar. It was the *correctness* of the sentences that was emphasized, never their value as to meaning or desirability.

Every good teacher wants her pupils to have good language—the sort that will be useful under any and all circumstances. To reach this very worthy state, the child must first find language important, rewarding and very needful to him. Since his first introduction to language (outside the family) is in the nurseries and preschool, these are the places where he must be given the right foundation— and the language he does acquire must be a *child's* language. When asked his age, for example, he should be taught to say, "Five," or "I'm five." The formal response, "I am five years old," is anything but childlike. The good preschool teacher will want to see that her pupils are able to communicate in the vernacular of their peers. She will want her children to use language as the natural expression of all they think, feel and do, and to look upon the lipreading of language as a means of knowing what other people think, feel and do.

There can be no greater reward and no keener delight than that which comes to the preschool teacher of a group of chattering, busy, happy and learning five-year-olds.

CHAPTER IV

LEARNING BY DOING

Yet all experience is an arch where through
Gleams that untraveled world.

ALFRED LORD TENNYSON
Ulysses

WHEN a deaf child leaves the preschool class at the age of six or six-and-a-half he should have a very real sense of the meaning and use of words in all his relationships with people both at home and in school. He should be able to work in a group, at least for periods of twenty minutes or longer, depending upon the length of time his interest is sustained. The interests and activities of the six-year-old are much broader and in many ways vastly different than they were when the child was five.

In this book I have been trying to describe the developmental steps of language growth. Naturally each deaf child proceeds at his own rate of speed, and not all children of any particular age will fit exactly into the program as I am describing it for the age in question. In this chapter I am talking about the six-year-old deaf child who has had the benefit of nursery and preschool training. In many schools this will not be so, since some children will not be entering school until they have reached the age of five or six. Yet if the teacher bears in mind, in dealing with these children, the fact that their feelings and interests are the same as any five- or six-year-old, even though their language may not be developed to a very great extent, she will still be able to make use of the suggestions given in this chapter as well as in previous chapters.

The language of the child of six or seven should be functional and should be brought into use whenever circumstances dictate. At this age children who have moved through a nursery and pre-school program should be able to take part in class discussions about themselves and their activities and should comprehend a great deal of the language used to and by six-year-olds. It is well to keep in mind the fact that understanding language is a simpler process than using it—and always comprehension must come before use, as we have said before. Little hearing children comprehend language far beyond their ability to use it. They are given time and opportunity to grow in the use of language and just so must the deaf be given time and opportunity, plus wise teaching.

Children in the first year of "real school" are bound to have many ideas to express and they should be given the language to do so and the opportunities to make this language their own eventually. They are going to need many new words if they are to make themselves known and understood. Their vocabularies should grow by leaps and bounds. They generally do if the atmosphere of the classroom is conducive to lively interests, love of communication and happy, satisfying group activities. The vocabulary of a child can grow only through use and should become part and parcel of the whole child—his thinking, wishing and planning. It should be an outlet for his many activities. If vocabulary is acquired by memorizing long lists of new words, the teacher cannot rightly feel satisfied. Her pupils may know words, but they will have no idea of how to use them. Words learned out of context have little meaning or value to the deaf child. He should add to his vocabulary as the hearing do, through need for self-expression, understanding and unending assistance.

The great emphasis in Lower School I is still to be placed on speech, lipreading, silent reading, and language, though the class will also do much more in the preparation for manuscript writing. At the Lexington School the children do not actually start to write until the second half of the year and often not until after the spring vacation. When they do start, they write their own little stories and news items of a few sentences each. Prior to this they have mastered the technique of writing in manuscript form and have learned to look up the spelling of words in the various classroom and teacher-made dictionaries. When they start to write they have a purpose in doing so.

The reason for postponing the use of writing by these children until the latter part of the year, rather than stressing it in the early months of the term, is that we wish to stress *oral* language—discussions, conversations and talks about activities. At our school the first grade is still a program of broad stimulation in order to give experiences and provoke observation and thinking as the groundwork for language growth. (This is especially important for children who have not had nursery and preschool experience.) The difference between preschool and the first grade of the lower school is actually one of degree. The programs are largely the same, but first grade children are ready to absorb more, and to be held responsible for more.

The first few weeks of this new school adventure should be a review of what was done in the preschool, a period of orientation to a new class and teacher, a time of adjustment to a new regime. Getting acquainted before starting on the stepped-up program is a sound idea and brings worthwhile dividends. During these early weeks the teacher is able to discover the individual needs of each child in the class. During this time the children become familiar with the way in which the teacher talks to them, what she expects in the way of conformity, what things she likes and what her classroom interests and enthusiasms are. The atmosphere of a classroom is usually indicative of the quality of work being accomplished and the satisfaction of both teacher and pupils in their work. An atmosphere that is relaxed, constructive and conducive to growth should be established during the first few weeks of the school session. Much new language is bound to be introduced during this getting-acquainted time, for talking is being done by children and teacher alike as new experiences arise and as new playtime activities are introduced, new trips taken, new stories told, new books obtained from the library for the classroom reading table, new art materials discovered, new rhythms learned.

All during this time the teacher should be making mental note of the particular questions to be emphasized, the expressions most often called for, the vocabulary needs of the group, the speech needs (new elements as well as those previously stressed), and the particular language needs.

The vocabulary and language of the class should emerge from all the varied interests and activities engaged in throughout the year. Out of each activity should grow some particular concept of the world (from a child's point of view), some new words, some everyday expressions, some needed questions associated with the activity, and most important of all, the beginnings of a language pattern. For example—one of the means through which wide language growth will be stimulated would be through a daily discussion of some item of interest or some event in the personal life of

Date	Date	Date
Janice	Bobby	Vickie

I am going to visit my grandmother on Saturday. I have a present for her.	Daddy will take me to the zoo next Sunday. We will see the baby bear.	Yesterday Jean and I played house with our dolls. We were mothers. We had a lovely time.

Date	Date	Date	Date
Susie	Johnny	Jean	David

I'm going to Bloomingdale's after school. Mother is going to buy me some new shoes. I'm so happy.	I was lucky this morning. I found a nickel on the sidewalk. I'll put it in my bank.	My little cousin is staying at my house. I play with her at night.	Thursday is my birthday. I'll be seven years old. I'll have a party.

Seven-year-olds make news.

each child. This activity is commonly identified as "news" work. If properly conducted the news period can be an excellent language activity at this level because it makes use of personal experiences and ideas of the children, it allows for needed repetition and places emphasis on ordinary, everyday language. All little children love to talk about themselves and their doings and to do so requires a usable vocabulary. One way to do this is through discussion of news.

The teacher tapes a large sheet of newsprint on the blackboard. A child tells her what day and date to put on the sheet (using black crayon). Then various news items are presented by the children. When a child has the floor the others should watch to see what he is saying. I was delighted to hear a child say, "Everybody look at me. My news is different today." The teacher must, in the beginning, give a great deal of help to the child speaking. In doing so she should indirectly make clear to the other children what is being

39

said. If the news isn't really newsworthy it is not written on the sheet, but when a child gives something of interest it is written down. In the early part of the year the news items are very simple, even with help from the teacher. Examples of news given by pupils follow:

> Susie's mother bought her a new dress. It is pretty.
> We went to the pet shop. We bought two fish.
> Johnny didn't come to school today. He is sick.

Note the use of contractions. I feel that children should be given common contractions along with the tenses as they are acquired—did not—didn't, is not—isn't, will not—won't.

As children master simple forms of expression they learn other ways of saying the same thing: "Johnny didn't come to school yesterday because he was sick. We are sorry."

Gradually, as their ideas become more complex, the teacher can provide them with more advanced vocabulary and language forms. Their news will now become more colorful and interesting: "Johnny is absent again today. We are sorry he is sick. Maybe we'll write a letter to him." Other examples of news are:

> Susie's father went away on an airplane last night. He flew to Florida. He'll come back next week.
> Jean played with her cousin after school yesterday. They played hopscotch and Jean won.
> Johnny found a nickel this morning. He's going to put it in his bank.

These sheets of daily news are kept together and children refer to them frequently. In addition to the bare language facts the children learn much incidental language, as the following illustrations will show:

> Vickie went to the hospital after school yesterday. Bobby went, *too*.
> Janice didn't go to the park last Sunday. Mary didn't go *either*.
> Johnny had to stay in the house because he had a cold. He played games and had fun *anyhow*.

At some time during the day the teacher should write the individual news of each child on a blackboard, always reserving the same space for the same pupil. She should write just what the child says and what he would write himself if he were able to do so.

At a later period each child selects someone to read his news and as this is done the teacher changes the pronouns and verbs. She uses yellow chalk to make the changes stand out. The news would look like this.

Janice is
~~I~~   ~~Am~~ going to visit ~~my~~ grandmother on Saturday.

She has
~~I~~ ~~have~~ a present for her.

Bobby's   him
      Daddy will take ~~me~~ to the zoo next Sunday.

They
~~We~~ will see the baby bear.

                         Vickie   their
      Yesterday Jean and ~~I~~   played house with ~~our~~

        They   They
dolls. ~~We~~ were mothers. ~~We~~ had a lovely time.

To be sure the children need a great deal of help in making these changes at first, but in a month or two they are able to make most of them orally without too much help. By midyear many of the children find it quite natural to use the proper pronoun, verb tense, or singular or plural forms in communications of all kinds. I have seen first-grade children become very conscious of what verb tense is needed to make their language correct, or what particular pronoun is required to make what they are trying to say clear and definite. Children can become "language conscious" if they are taught to use words and language constructions through constant, repetitive, meaningful communication.

The teacher must give the correct language to the child over and over and over again. She cannot let any errors pass. She must make these corrections patiently, helpfully and always in a spirit of cooperation. The child must sense the need of help and accept it willingly, happily and often. It makes a great difference in the acceptance of repeated corrections and reminders if a child knows and can see the value of them as a means of furthering greater facility in the use of communication.

There is very little stimulation or interest to children in a news period where a child tells a bit of news and immediately finds himself replaced by another child. That kind of procedure can be dull,

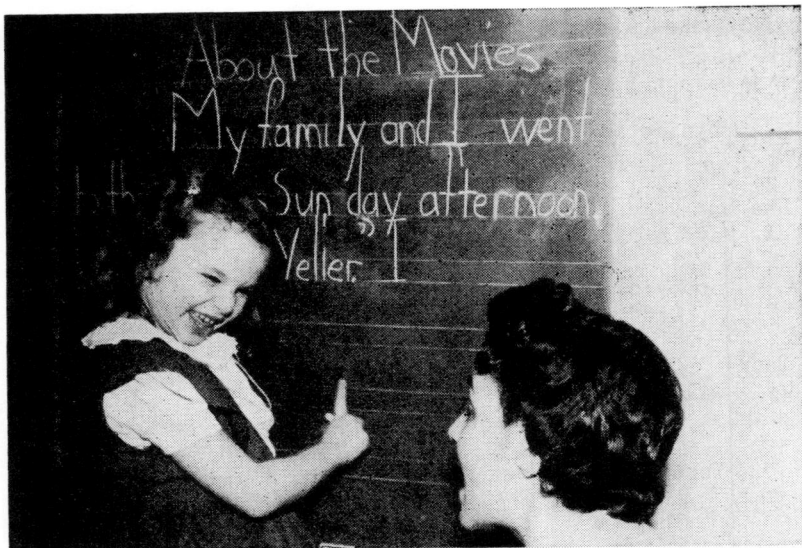

Photo by Norman Crane

Language can be fun.

automatic and not worth very much in the way of growth in language. The entire class should be interested in what the child who "has the floor" is saying, and if the members of the class have any ideas about the matter or want the subject clarified, a discussion should ensue.

Let us take Janice's news. When she was telling it one child said, "Why the present?" The teacher helped him say, "Why are you giving your grandmother a present?" Janice replied, "It's her birthday." Bobby said, "What is the present?" Soon all queries were satisfied!

For Bobby's news the question came out, "Who told you there was a baby bear?" One child remarked, "Be careful of the mother bear!"

When Vickie told her news two youngsters joined in the conversation—Bobby: "I don't like to play house." Susie: "Did you wear your mother's dress or shoes?"

David's news was of extreme interest. Were his mother and sisters coming to the party? Would there be ice cream and a birthday cake? Who would come? What games would be played? Of course, the teacher had to help with these questions, but that did not lessen the interest. It takes much longer to handle this kind of news period, but the time devoted to it is well spent.

The news period is much more than just telling of something that has happened or will happen. Through the medium of news the children learn many things—as, for example:

New vocabulary—nouns, verbs, adjectives, adverbs.

Use of pronouns—those they need to know at this period.

Verb tenses—those most often required at this level.

Conjunctions—and, but, so, because.

Singular and plurals of everyday usable nouns.

Prepositions—those used normally by any six-year-old.

Punctuation—comma, period, question mark, exclamation point.

Use of capital letters.

Time phrases—those dealing with "time elements" as six-year-olds need them. Yesterday, today, tomorrow, tonight, last night, last week, a long time ago, in December (or any month), on Tuesday (or any day) and many others. No formal calendar work is given.

Idiomatic expressions—My goodness!, Well, well!, O.K., That's all right, and many others.

Questions—any questions that children want to ask about the news should be formulated for them.

It has never seemed to me wise or necessary for a deaf child to have to learn all the pronouns at one fell swoop, nor should he learn all the nominative pronouns, then the objective pronouns, then the possessive pronouns, and last of all the reflexive pronouns. Many a child who has memorized such lists can reel them off without error and yet lack the ability to use them correctly in oral or written language. Little children, deaf or hearing, need a great deal of practice in the use of correct pronouns. They have use for some nominative, some objective, some possessive and some reflexive pronouns, but they do not need all of them and I see no need for the pronouns to be presented in columns. Day-by-day use in understood situations will eventually give all children a correct concept of the meaning and use of pronouns in self-expression. Children who learn in this way will not be found still misusing pronouns in the middle or upper school.

It is often very fascinating to hear little hearing children misuse pronouns in their early years. A number of years ago I was a guest at the Rhode Island School for the Deaf and my host's young hearing daughter waited to escort me downstairs to breakfast. As we neared the dining room she called out gaily, "Here we come, both of them." Many a little child misuses pronouns until constant repetition of the correct one finally "takes" and the child no longer has any difficulty. But drill is of no value unless it makes *sense* to the child.

I knew a little eight-year-old deaf boy who was in a class where letters were written home every Friday. For weeks the children had written, "We wrote letters to our mothers." This little boy used the pronoun *we* as a memory gem, but he had no concept of its real meaning. When he was in the hospital he wrote a card to his teacher and said, "Dear Miss P., I am sick. I want we to write a letter to me." He had had repetition, but it was not very practical for him.

This little boy was no great exception. Far too many deaf children use language they have been told is right although they have no concept of its true meaning.

In the same way I feel definitely that children should absorb the meaning of various verb tenses through *use* and not spend time on forms alone. Conjugations have no place in the teaching of language to any little children, deaf or hearing. The only tenses to be stressed should be those for which the children have need in their oral and, in time, written work. Children of six or seven do not speak as adults and do not require a knowledge of all forms and tenses of verbs. Some verbs naturally will be used mostly in the present tense. Even then not all the forms will be used. Verbs such as *have, be, think, hope, want* and *like* are used most frequently in the present tense. Such verbs as *go, see, buy, make* and *ride,* and countless other "doing" verbs, will be needed in the past or future tenses. Children require so much repetition in the handling of the needed verb forms that those should be the ones most often emphasized. However, children in any grade should always be given the correct form needed at the moment to express clearly what is in their minds. If some child definitely needs the present progressive of a verb to express himself correctly, it should be given to him with a simple explanation. I do not think that he should be exposed, in the first grade, to a thorough teaching of the present progressive tense of all the verbs he knows in the past tense, but I do believe that in the instances where that tense is called for the teacher should give it to him.

The children inevitably will need to use some verbs in the past negative or the past interrogative. These tenses should again be learned through use—not by means of conjugation. Teachers do not need to fear that children in the first year of school will get confused by this approach. They will not if, as they use verbs to express themselves, they understand the meaning of the various forms *and* are given continual opportunities to make the use of verbs important to them in their daily activities.

Much can be learned through the writing of day-to-day happenings if the teacher knows how to make the most of them, and the children should not be limited to the writing of "news." Notes, the planning for trips, parties, shows and visits all provide ammunition for the learning of new language and the practice of already learned expressions. Children in our first-year class always send me a "class project" note when they want to do something special or go out on some trip. There is always conversation about what is to be put into these notes which, by the way, are written by the teacher on newsprint, just as the news is done at the first part of the year.

One morning I was passing the room during the preparation of such a note and I heard the teacher say, "Are we going to *tell* Dr. Groht something or are we going to *ask* her something? What are we going to say in the letter?" A child volunteered, "May we go on the ferry?" "That's right," said the teacher, "we're going to ask her a question. I think we might ask, 'May we go for a ride on the ferry?' " From this simple discussion the children were beginning to comprehend the difference between *asking* and *telling*. Were they learning all about direct and indirect discourse? Of course not, but they were paving the way for such a study much later on. I might add here that these children often attempt to use *told* in a simple way and frequently tell of something mother or daddy has told them. (Mother told me that she saw Daddy in his office yesterday.) This is a limited use of the verb, but it is a small beginning and will help when the child needs to extend his knowledge of the verbs *ask, say* and *tell*.

Another way of using language is the telling of two- or three-sentence stories. Children enjoy doing this and they get practice in using necessary language forms. Tales about children, pets, trips, surprises, visitors and the like are of interest to the children and they enjoy making up these stories. These are told orally to the class and, if desired, written by the teacher. A few examples of stories by six-year-olds are:

A FUNNY DOG

Scotty was a little black dog. He was very fat. He looked funny when he walked. Everybody laughed at him.

NATURAL LANGUAGE FOR DEAF CHILDREN

A BIG DOG

Johnny was a little boy. He had a very big dog. One day the big dog chased a very little puppy. Johnny was cross. He said, "Don't do that."

MARY'S DOG

Mary had a cute dog. He could stand up. One day he pretended to dance. Mary laughed at him. She gave him something to eat.

The children should choose their own titles and think up their own stories. The teacher will have to help them with the language when they cannot put their ideas into words. The *point* of the stories is to encourage the imagination, bring out ideas and make use of language. Once the stories have been discussed and enjoyed they should be dropped, although on occasion, if some story pleased everyone, it might be written on a sheet of newsprint and kept for further reading.

Stories told by the teacher and dramatized by the pupils afford opportunity for the lipreading of new language and for the use of language by the children. A clever teacher can weave into her stories situations which will require the children to use conversational language in their dramatizations.

Teachers of six-, seven- and eight-year-olds should be able to think up endless numbers of stories revolving around the interests and experiences of their pupils. There should be a great deal of talking in a first-year class, and as the year goes on the children should contribute more and more to this talk. Six-year-olds have much to talk about!

Other means of using verbal English can be found in the play periods. Children love to play store or house, to pretend to go marketing, to act as a nurse, doctor, waitress, policeman, fireman, bus driver, clown, zookeeper, peanut man, mother, father, teacher or housekeeper. Learning what to say during these activities will give added opportunity for repetition and practice in the use of language.

All language given to a deaf child must represent the child's own thinking, feeling, experiencing. It is well for the teacher to bear in mind continually the fact that a child may think a thing very important, even though it is not so to the teacher's way of thinking.

No language written by teacher or pupil should ever be memorized and reproduced. If the children have learned a thing they should remember it. Children who have been taught to be responsible should and will profit by all teaching and correction.

In a group where there are children who need a more structured approach to the learning of some of the more difficult verbs—*to be* and *to have* in the present tense, for example—the teacher should plan periods of concentrated work on these forms. She should bear in mind that her aim is to teach the child to *use* these verbs and not just understand them. My objection to the use of elliptical sentences for practice in verb forms, or in any language construction, is that they do not allow for the child's using the verb in sentences of his own. Elliptical sentences represent the teacher's thoughts or ideas. They are her words. They may show the child that with certain pronouns we use *has* in the singular, but they do not provide opportunity for him to use the verb to express an idea. It is just as easy and much more beneficial to give the child exercises that will make him use the verb in expressing a complete thought that he will find useful outside of school. Telling about some of the things each child has (and I mean possesses, not just holds temporarily) will allow for seven or eight sentences. Such a lesson does not have to be stereotyped. The teacher, without taking undue time, can make the lesson both interesting and alive.

If Vickie says, "I have a dime," the teacher can add, "My goodness, that's a lot of money!" If Johnny says, "I have a new book," she can add, "Good, we'll read it after lunch." For repetition in using *has* the children can tell what other people actually have— "Daddy has a car." "Mommy has a new hat." "Jean has a big doll." "I have long, brown hair." For plural forms, they can tell what the nursery babies have—"The babies have many toys." "They have big blocks."—or what the boys have, or the girls have.

Pictures provide many opportunities for repetition in the use of language principles. Large or small pictures mounted on oak tag —pictures in books, magazines and on the walls—pictures drawn or painted by the children—all can be used for practice purposes, but they must be chosen carefully, with definite aims in view. If the verb *to have* is to be stressed the pictures chosen should clearly indicate use for that verb and should not be cluttered up with too many other possibilities. A set of pictures of babies, each having some object, can be used as an introduction. The teacher may say: "I have some lovely pictures of babies. You'll like them. I'll keep one picture and I'll give each of you one. Don't show your picture because we're going to talk about them first. Now we each have a baby. I'll tell about my baby first." She looks at the picture, "My baby's cute. She has a bottle." Then going round the class she says, "Bobby, what does your baby have?" He replies, "My baby has an orange." Then each child takes a turn. For review the pictures can be placed on the blackboard ledge and each baby given a name. Children can then say, or write if they know how, what each baby has. At a later time a set of pictures of girls or boys can be used— "This little girl has a Teddy." "This little boy has a bike." For use of the plural forms pictures of groups can be used. Always the teacher must keep the lesson alive through her own enthusiasm and her contributions to the conversation.

The same type of practice can be found for repetition of the forms of the verb *to be*. Talking about colors, sizes, weights and shapes will multiply the uses of the verb—"The rubber doll is little." "The rag doll is big." "This box is heavy." "Mary's ball is soft." "Cookies are good to eat." "The plates are round."

In general I believe that any work done to reinforce language usage should be carried on in as informal a way as possible, with the emphasis being on the *use* of the language rather than on the exercise. There must be meaning to the lesson. The children should be as interested in *what* they are saying as they are in *how* they are saying it. Good questions for the teacher to ask herself are: "Will what I am doing here have a carry-over outside this classroom? Is the child going to need this work? Is it helping him to grow mentally, making him really think things through?" Teachers need to check and evaluate their teaching constantly. If they do, they will be less likely to get into a rut and will find teaching a pleasure rather than a hard task.

Many trips should be taken. Sometimes these may be just walks around the neighborhood, looking in store windows, watching men excavating for a building, watching people (policeman, postman, bus driver, fireman), observing street scenes. Sometimes they may be planned trips on boats, trains, or buses. They should be trips to places of interest to children—out to the country, off to the beach, out to a farm, around the city, over bridges, under bridges, to railroad stations, to parks, playgrounds, picnic areas and, if available, to children's museums. The lipreading that is done, the information gained, the vocabulary acquired, and the experiences provided all make such out-of-school excursions well worth the time, effort and money spent on them. The value is inestimable so far as language is concerned. An example follows:

SHOPPING FOR A PUMPKIN

All the children went out to buy a pumpkin for Halloween. They went to many grocery stores, and they saw many pumpkins. One was too tall. One was too small. One was too fat. One was too flat. One was lopsided.

At last they found one that was just right. It was a nice, round orange pumpkin.

The children took turns carrying the pumpkin back to school.

Visitors to the classroom also help to widen the horizons of young deaf children and give them an ever-expanding knowledge of persons and places. First-grade children at Lexington School have a large map of the United States and a large globe in their schoolroom. They love to use these to find places where people come from, and they like to know how long it took them to get to New York. They have deduced, by themselves, that flying from one place to another is faster than traveling by train, that one can't walk to places that are very far from home, that people must buy plane, railroad or steamer tickets.

Visitors also afford many opportunities for the use of questions. Our first-graders ask such questions as the following:

What's your name?
Where do you live?
Did you come by plane? by train? by boat?
Do you live very far away?
Are you a teacher? a nurse? a doctor?
Are you married?
How many children do you have?
What are their names?
How old are they?
Are they deaf?
Why did you come to see us?
Do you like New York?
How long did it take to get here?

These questions grew gradually. The children themselves wanted to ask visitors if they were married so that they could tell whether to use "Miss" or "Mrs." in saying or writing the name. They were a bit puzzled as to what to do if a woman used "Dr." One youngster suggested they could look to see if she were wearing a wedding ring. The questions are not asked in any set order and on occasion only a few are asked. It depends very much on the visitors and how they respond to the children. This should not be a question-and-answer lesson! It should be more of a get-acquainted time. When a visitor said she lived in Pittsburgh seven-year-old Vickie said, "I lived there when I was small." On one occasion there was a visitor from South America, and Susie told him that her father was down there at that time. Millie told a doctor that her daddy was a doctor, too.

I'd like to cite an incident that amused the visitors very much and showed that the children really did think about what was being said. Bobby said to one woman in the group, "Are you married?" When she replied in the negative, Janice said, "That's too bad." To make things seem better, Johnny said, "Maybe after awhile."

Children should think through both question and answer. A child who was told that a woman was not married was promptly chided by the rest of the class when she asked, "Have you any children?" There must always be a purpose in using questions—the purpose being to get information. The information thus gained should be used for further verbal thought and expression. Allowing children to ask pointless questions, just to give them practice in using a question form, will not be of any value when they really want to find out something.

Many everyday expressions should be added to those used by pre-school pupils. They should be in use whenever situations call for them. Perhaps some needed expressions might be: "How do you spell that?" "May I have a turn?" "It's my turn next." "May I come after John?" "I have one, thank you." "I can write that." "Have you any?" "I can't find it." "I'll try." "That's wonderful!" "Goody!" "Never mind, it's all right."

Children who have the habit of talking, not only to the teacher and not merely on request, should make use of many such expressions in the classroom and anywhere else they may be. Speaking in connected language must become habitual if it is to be of help to the deaf child. The habit of using language naturally has to be started in the early grades. The pattern for language work should be well established in the first and second grades. If the children in these classes have the right attitude toward language, if they *think* in language—not gestures—if they look upon it as a medium of communicating thought rather than as an exercise and if they consider language a natural approach to pleasant relationships with others, they will attempt to use language under all circumstances.

There are children with normal intelligence who need more time than a school year to achieve the results desired for first-graders. Why this should be so is a moot question! Teachers have always wondered why children of like ability in the same class with the same teacher and the same opportunities for development, do not all proceed at the same rate. The causes for this may vary from psychological reasons to variations in the home background, all of which must be taken into account in evaluating a child's progress. Is it not so with hearing classes? In most first- and second-year classes in schools for the hearing, that I know anything about, the children are divided into two and often three sections. Group I may be far ahead of Group II or III in reading in particular, and usually in other subjects as well. No attempt is made by the teachers of these classes to insist that each child in a class of thirty or more pupils read at the same rate and cover the same material in the same length of time. The teacher of experience knows that there will be some in Group II who will move up to Group I in due time, and some who will need a longer time to cover the work.

Even in a well-graded class of deaf children the teacher will, perforce, have to adapt her teaching to accommodate individual differences. She may need to groom the very gifted child for a more advanced group, and she may have to plan some repetition for the child not quite up to the rest of the class.

It is my belief that no child, put in a certain group in September, should have to remain in that group until June if careful study indicates that he does not belong there. Time is as precious a commodity to the deaf child as it is to anyone else. It should not be wasted.

The language arts (language, lipreading, speech and reading) must be emphasized continuously in the first few years of school. On a child's ability to use language correctly and with comprehension will hang his success or failure throughout his school life.

I would like to make it clear that the teachers of our preschool, first and second grades do have a plan for working on the language arts—a plan that they evolve from the daily lives of their pupils. It is "child initiated," but nonetheless a satisfactory plan because it is bound to provide an outlet for the teaching of the language arts. What the children tell any one of these teachers on a Monday morning may form the framework for all of a teacher's weekly plan. If new experiences have arisen, new things have been seen, bought or handled over the week-end, if new ideas have come up, the teacher may want to continue stressing these things at every opportunity during the week. She will have to judge whether these needs are temporary or whether they will be lasting. If, for instance, most of the little girls returned to school with new spring outfits and are excited about them, it might lead the teacher to discuss clothes—winter clothes, spring clothes, party clothes. She might talk about seasons, or places where different types of clothes are worn, or clothes for trips, or materials from which clothes are made. A trip might be taken to look at department store windows where spring clothes are displayed. The children could tell which dresses or coats or hats they liked or disliked. During the week the teacher might tell a few stories revolving around new clothes—situations about a new dress and a jar of paint, a new suit and a wire fence, a lovely hat and a beautiful dress that matched it, a little child and new shiny shoes. All of these things could be used to get in needed verbs, nouns, adjectives and phrases.

In addition the teacher would continue in the week's plan to work on all the language of everyday importance that she has been stressing right along. She would add numbers and names of colors to those already learned. She might plan a class note to a parent, an absent pupil, a supervising teacher, a child in the school infirmary, or some other person for whom a composite note might be in order. To a good teacher, everything is grist for the mill. She will not allow opportunities for teaching new language or reviewing old language to pass by the board.

There may be some weeks when the teacher's plan can be carefully and consistently carried out, and others when she has to make changes. A skillful teacher will be able to do this in a way that will be productive of real learning. A teacher once said to me, "A teacher can't go wrong in ———— School because she knows every day of every week what she is to teach in the way of nouns, verbs, adjectives and so on." My answer was, "To my way of thinking she couldn't possibly go right!" What would such a teacher do about some noun or verb screaming to be taught because of the children's need at that particular point in their lives? If not taken, the right and reasonable opportunity may not present itself again —the eagerness may be gone.

What would she do, for instance, if someone came in to tell or show her something? One day I had a letter from a six-year-old niece who wrote, "I have a rabbit. I named him 'Thumper' because he thumps when he runs." Immediately the children wanted to know what "thump" meant. They wanted to know if kittens "thumped" or did they run softly and lightly? They wanted to show how they thought "Thumper" ran. This sort of thing is indigenous to normal childhood, and young deaf pupils are normal children.

How would the teacher from ———— School have handled this situation?

If a teacher "inherits" a class that has few ideas, she will have to see to it that the pupils do have things to think about and talk about. She will have to find interests, experiences and conditions that will call forth ideas on the part of the children and lead them to think about these things in terms of language. Little children love to be with people who love them sincerely, who are wholly interested in what they do and what happens to them, who can meet them on their own level when that is called for. A "must" for every teacher of deaf children is an insight into the nature and needs of these children and a deeper insight into their mental make-up. Without this insight she will be unable to help her charges to grow "in wisdom and stature, and in favour with God and man." (Luke 2:52)

CHAPTER V

NEW WORLDS TO EXPLORE

Every day is a fresh beginning,
Every morn is the world made new.

SARAH CHAUNCEY WOOLSEY
New Every Morning

IN ANY classroom and in any grade, each day should definitely start off with friendly, sometimes lively conversation—not only morning greetings. As children progress from grade to grade they should take an increasingly larger part in the morning exchange of interesting accounts of what has occurred, been seen or observed since the preceding day. Also during this period of just *talking,* plans for projected trips or activities can be thoroughly discussed. The resultant language growth from this daily conversation time is very great. Those taking part grow more and more verbally communicative, not only with their teachers but with all with whom they have contact.

This is a time when the child, be he young or teen-age, can express himself, reveal his interests, unburden his mind and at the same time learn to respect the opinions of others, share in their interests and help in their perplexities. This is a time for stimulating the child to express himself orally, to think things through, to learn to expand his thinking beyond himself and his personal problems. Deaf children *need* to learn to think beyond themselves.

The amount of time devoted to the morning conversational periods should depend upon the particular interests of the day. Some days may be more important than others and the conversation may last a half hour or longer. On other days there may be less to talk about and the time spent in doing so may be not more than ten or fifteen minutes. Much depends upon the attitude of the teacher and the extent to which she is really interested in what transpires outside her classroom and in what her pupils are thinking or feeling.

All children like to exchange thoughts and information and want to have someone to talk to. They also want to have the right words to clothe their thoughts. It is often during the opening "give and take" conversation that the teacher can discover language needs and follow them up with more direct teaching later in the day. At this time she can give the children many idiomatic expressions and responses to remarks—an acquisition of importance to any deaf pupil of any age. It is depressing to have a deaf boy respond to a general observation such as, "I love a day like this!" with the one word, "Yes." Why not teach him the proper responses? That boy could have said, "I do, too!" or "So do I!" or even, "Me, too!" A deaf girl who was hurrying along a corridor and bumped into a teacher also said, "Yes," when the teacher remarked, "You seem to be in a hurry!" That girl lacked the ability to respond. She might have said, "I'm late for class," or given whatever reason was in order. At one time, when a teacher had been ill, I said to the class, "Miss ———— is better and she'll be back tomorrow." It was certainly rewarding to have these responses: "That's good." "I'm glad to hear that." "That's wonderful news." "Please tell her we'll be happy to see her." There was no dearth of adequate responses in that room because those children had had several years of daily morning conversational periods.

There have been countless hundreds of instances where deaf children, and not only young ones, have responded with meaningless monosyllables because they had not been taught what to say. This lack should be overcome and one way is to have the morning exchange of ideas. People often stand out as interesting, stimulating, attractive personalities because they have the gift of outgoing responses.

Deaf children, accustomed to oral speech and language, will learn much from the daily chitchat of normal verbal conversation. This talk, however, cannot be stilted and formal. It must be free and easy, with the accent on content as well as expression.

There definitely should be stimulating talk at the beginning of the school day in a class of seven- and eight-year-olds. The news that the day pupils bring to school can be varied, exciting, funny, important or informative. Resident pupils also should have things to tell—a letter or package from home, a trip to a shop or other place with a counselor, new games played, happenings in the playroom or yard, articles brought in, visits to the infirmary, and the various school activities such as swimming, Brownie meetings, movies, shows put on by the children themselves, and many other

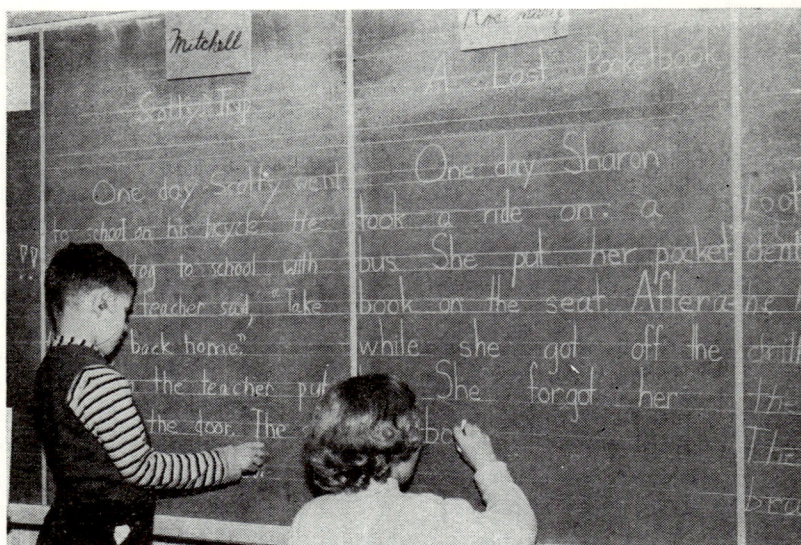

Seven- and eight-year-olds express themselves.

subjects of conversation. Generally the problem for the teacher here, especially if she has an up-and-coming class, is to keep the talk well in tow. The conversation should never get out of hand. At this age each child wants to have his say as soon as he comes in. I have seen children start to tell the teacher something before they got into the room or before they had removed their outdoor clothing. It is always a pleasure to see children gathered about their teacher, talking about whatever has taken place since they last met.

During the conversation it may help if use is made of the blackboard for writing a new word or name or idiomatic expression. At times a hasty bit of sketching by teacher or child will clarify meanings. The teacher should not make this period a *lesson* time. She should be as informal as possible, be pleasantly surprised or interested, add her own feelings and ideas in simple language, and make the children feel happy and contented about the beginning of a day in school.

In addition to the value of getting such a good daily start, the children get a great deal of practice in casual lipreading which is what does them the most good outside the school. They learn to read the lips unconsciously when they are vitally interested in what is being said. The more of this type of lipreading deaf children get *in* the classroom, the better mixers they will be when outside it—the better will be their relations with hearing people and the better adjusted they themselves will be.

Very often the teacher will find suggestions for daily news articles, "short short stories" or silent reading materials from the things discussed in the early conversations. She may say to a child, "That was very interesting. Why don't you write about it in your news later on?" To another child she might say, "You could write a cute little story about that!" Again, she may discover a need for certain questions and make a mental note to do some concentrated work on them. She may feel that the children as a group need to add certain words, phrases or idioms to their vocabularies. These ideas for planning a daily program are a by-product of the morning conversation period, though not the primary reason for it.

The language arts will continue to receive the predominating emphasis in this grade. The work in speech will cover much more in the knowledge of speech sounds, pronunciations and all the techniques of good production. The children should be held responsible for using all the speech sounds they know and for trying at all times to speak carefully and intelligibly. Great strides should be made in reading during the year. The teacher should stress the use of teacher-made material, readers, simple textbooks on social studies, and library books. Auditory training should be enriched through language growth and, where children can profit from it, a full and meaningful program should be developed.

Since these children have learned to write, their news should be written by them after they have told it orally. When one child's news is read by another child, the latter should make the necessary changes from first to third person in the pronouns. If other phrases need changing, he should do that, too. For the first half of the year these changes should be made in writing, but in the second half they can well be done orally.

It is a good plan to give a title to the news a child writes because this helps him to stick to the point. At first the teacher may have to suggest a title, but very soon the child will think of his own. As soon as children are able to write any type of composition (news, letters, stories) they should be taught to paragraph. Deaf children, just as much as hearing children, need to be taught the habit of speaking and writing about one thing at a time.

The writing of news is of value to the deaf child because this type of language work provides the child with the vocabulary he needs for everyday living, but it should not be run into the ground. Seven-

57

and eight-year-olds profit from this kind of language work but beyond this age children should not write daily news. Perhaps for them the writing of week-end news would be more to the point. There are many other types of composition and these should be more often in use.

Children should not write long, drawn-out news items. It is a good habit to develop early the idea that quality is more desirable than quantity. The child should tell the interesting things he has done and not be allowed to write day after day about the same routine, daily doings. He must know the difference between what is and what is not worth writing about. He should feel that he is writing for someone else to read, not for practice in the use of language. There is a vast difference in the attitude of a child who thinks he *has* to write some news "or else," and the child who wants to write because he is bubbling over with things he wants to tell. In a well-conducted class the news period can be of very real value to the pupils, and there should always be strong motivation for it.

On occasions where the entire class has had the same experience and all want to tell about it, the teacher might, after a class discussion of the experience, suggest titles for each child. Let us say the children have spent the previous afternoon in the park. To have each pupil try to write about everything that was seen or done would make for very long, rambling compositions. The teacher might assign such titles as "At the Zoo," "The Funny Monkey," "The Peanut Man," "The Polar Bears," "Fun on the Playground." Then each child could write a short and worthwhile account of one phase of the outing.

Personally I prefer short compositions because first of all they are individual. Each child tells about what interests him. We should not expect all the children to be impressed by the same thing or even to see the same thing, and therefore we should not ask all children in a class to think alike or write alike about a given experience. Secondly, short compositions allow for the child's receiving proper explanation for whatever corrections are made and he will be more apt to remember these corrections. Thirdly, each child will profit by the reading and the corrections of all the compositions, though he will be held responsible only for his own. Children can imbibe much teaching by taking part in this sort of group activity. My fourth reason is that writing many short compositions is of more value than taking a great deal of time for one long one. In the latter case there is not time for real teaching and the teacher cannot cover the work of the entire class within a given period. A child who thinks he must write a long news account might resort to the use of news that is old and no longer of first importance, or he might incorporate into his writing unrelated sentences that he has used in other types of language work.

Examples of brief original compositions follow:

LETTERS TO SICK FRIENDS

Dear Lev,
I'm sorry that you are sick. Do you have the flu? That's too bad.
We changed our room around. We changed our blackboards, too.
I miss you. Hurry back to school.

Love,
Rosemary

STORIES

Doggie Friends　　　　　　　Sharon

Karen has two little doggie friends. One is called Doggy, and the other is called Petty. They went to the store to buy a pumpkin for Halloween.

In the Woods　　　　　　　Nancy

My daddy and I and my brother Douglas will go to the woods next Sunday. I'll look for some autumn leaves. Maybe I'll bring them to school.

Corrected news should never be memorized or reproduced. Once the experiences have been thoroughly discussed and written about, the incentive to tell satisfied, and the accounts read and perhaps commented upon by the rest of the class, there is no great value in having children memorize what they have written. They are not going to need the exact language again and there is no learning in such a procedure. I prefer that each pupil read over his corrected composition, note where he had had to be corrected and *why*—"Why did you need the past tense?" "Why did you need an *s* there?" On occasion a child might want to keep something he has written, and in such a case I should let him copy the material. To check on the children's learning I might sometimes say at a later time, "That was such interesting news everyone wrote this morning that I think your mothers would like to know about it. Let's write letters and put that news in them." If the child profited from his work in the morning he should be able to recall it in the afternoon. If he changes a word or phrase but does not alter the meaning I should accept that. If he *learned* the correct language to use he should be able to apply it any time and in any place. If he cannot, he will need further teaching and further repetition in its use.

A child will *think* if he is trained to do so. The teacher must constantly bear in mind the fact that learning involves understanding. The deaf child who memorizes and reproduces language he does not understand is not learning. The teacher must be sure that the child understands the language he is using and that what he writes has to do with perception of ideas and not with memory.

One caution when teaching paragraphing and sequence: A child who puts all the news in one paragraph because it occurred on one day, even though the facts are unrelated, should be shown why he is incorrect. For example he may write:

Harvey's father bought him a new bike yesterday. Mary broke her doll's head. She cried very hard.

He should be shown that although both things happened yesterday they do not belong in the same paragraph.

The writing of what I like to label "short short stories" is a very good way to bring in repeated use of language principles which the children need. Children love stories—those that are told to them, those that they read and those that they write, even though the latter may be extremely simple. Many stories should be written during the year—stories suggested by pictures, or experiences of one kind or another, or imaginative stories or what I call "toy stories."

Since play is known to be a factor in learning we should have more play in our efforts to teach language. This is the underlying principle of "toy stories." It has been said that play is the great integrating and developing force in childhood. Much of the hearing child's ability to use language is gained through his play activities. Play is really an attitude of mind, and language that is part of the child's play will prove satisfying and will be productive of desirable results. It is possible to teach the deaf child many language principles through the medium of play. Games, dramatizations, puzzles, pantomime and toy manipulations all offer possibilities for repetition of thought which the teacher wishes to impress upon the minds of the children. Along with play must come imagination—for imagination is a vital factor in learning. Deaf children are as full of imaginative ideas as are hearing youngsters. It is not necessary to be as literal with deaf children as has been thought.

Using tiny toy miniatures of real things, and telling stories with them is entertaining for little children. Using attractive and alluring little objects to give follow-up work on a language principle previously taught can call forth from children zest and keen desire to have a part in playing with these objects. To illustrate: A little village may be set up at one corner of a table and the children told, "This is a village." At the opposite corner of the table a miniature farm may be arranged and the remark made, "And this is a farm." The children quickly grasp the picture set up for them and love to name the tiny wooden dolls and animals and place the little buildings which are used for this kind of work. The teacher, moving the toy children and animals about, tells a story about some children who lived on a farm but went to school in a village, and what happened when their dog followed them. She may even tell two or three different stories having to do with the scene laid out on the the table. Soon there are cries of, "May I tell a story?" "Please let me tell a story next." "I have a good idea for a story."

Once children have had pleasure in listening to the teacher's stories and have tried some of their own, often with assistance to be sure, they will have just as much fun with a story structured to give repetition on some definite point in language. The setup can be so arranged and the story told by the teacher in such a way that the language principle she wants emphasized will appear over and over again. Let us suppose that the teacher wishes to get in some follow-up work on the preposition *behind*. She sets up a miniature park, true to life with trees, rocks, tiny zoo and little buildings. She puts down a little boy and two dogs. The children are charmed by the little park. The story might run along something like this:

One day John took Rags and Spot to the park. They were naughty! They ran away. (TEACHER *pretends to make the dogs run and then hides them.*) John wanted to find them. He looked *behind* a tree (TEACHER *walks* JOHN *over to a tree and pretends that he is searching behind it.*) but he didn't see them. Then he looked *behind* another tree. (JOHN *looks.*) He found Rags. Then John looked *behind* a big rock. Spot wasn't there. He looked *behind* a bush. No Spot! John was cross. At last he found Spot *behind* an old wagon. He took the dogs home and put them in their little yard. He told them they'd have to stay there because they had run away from him.

In all storytelling the animation of the teacher, and her dexterity in illustrating actions with the little toys, has much to do with the success of the operation. The children are usually fascinated by what is going on and their imaginations are stirred. It will be observed that the lipreading involved in such a story is quite simple and the repetition of the preposition not too tiresome. The children themselves will love to set up imaginary parks, streets, playgrounds, towns, beaches and various places familiar to them. They will enjoy making up their own stories and moving the little objects about as they tell what happened. Such an activity provides opportunity for practice in using not only prepositions but pronouns, verbs, adverbs and adjectives. Little toys suitable for this activity may be found in toy stores, stationers, and shops that sell favors and party materials. Miniature farms, villages and parks often come in net bags and can be found in many little shops catering to children.

On occasion the teacher might wish to have the children use more than one preposition. To attain this goal, she might suggest that the youngsters help in setting up a park or any desired place. The conversation would probably go like this:

TEACHER: "Where shall I put this tree?"
CHILD: *"Near* the big rock."
TEACHER: "That's a good place. Now where shall I put this little bench?"
CHILD: *"Under* the tree."
TEACHER: "How about this funny little building?"
CHILD: "I think, *in* the corner."

When the setup is completed, the teacher and the children can weave little stories about the things at hand. Such periods should be, as far as the children are concerned, just a happy time of relaxation and pleasure. They should come at odd times during the day or week and should be informal—the children and the teacher gathered around a table, enjoying themselves and yet thinking about what they are doing and saying.

Many of these stories can be written up by the children, and this provides material for compositions. Also, the children may think up some good stories and later enact them with the toys. These simple stories are what I mean by the "short short story." Of course not all stories should have the same treatment—some should be written and kept. Children could have notebooks called "My Own Story Book" or "My Short Short Stories" or "Stories I Like." In addition, stories can be written by the children for dramatization at the "relaxing" time of the day when they need a break from sitting still. Children have no trouble in visualizing chairs as trees and in impersonating animals or characters in a story. If wisely directed there will be increased motivation for all types of language work in all such activities.

Very often suggestions for writing short compositions will come from the children themselves. The teacher of a second-year class became aware of the need for work on the phrase *a piece of.* The children wanted to use it frequently. That seemed to be the right motivation for learning about partitives. Bringing in a birthday cake for one of the children, the teacher worked out with the class the difference between *a cake* and *a piece of cake.* The youngsters volunteered other information such as *a pie* and *a piece of pie, a loaf of bread* and *a piece of bread,* and gave several other illustrations of uses of the phrase. Later, the teacher talked about a little boy whose mother gave him *a piece of pie* and he dropped it on his nice clean suit, and about a little girl who found *a piece of pie* on the kitchen table and ate it all up and whose mother said, "Who ate my *piece of pie?*" All the children wanted to contribute stories about somebody and *a piece of pie.* The stories were short but good. These are samples written by children who were either eight or almost eight at the time:

JOHNNY AND THE PIE

Johnny's mother made a chocolate pie. She put it on a shelf. Johnny tried to get it. It fell on the floor. He said, "Oh, my!"

MRS. SMITH'S SURPRISE

Mrs. Smith wanted to surprise her family so she made a wonderful apple pie. At supper the family had the pie for dessert. Mr. Smith said, "This is a good piece of pie." Mrs. Smith felt happy.

PIE AND MILK

When Mary came home from school she saw a glass of milk and a piece of pumpkin pie on the kitchen table. She ate the piece of pie. It was good. She didn't drink the milk and her mother said, "You cannot have a piece of pie tomorrow."

These compositions, like all that are written in any grade, should follow ten or fifteen minutes of oral discussion during which time the children think out what they are going to say and get the spelling of a new word by looking it up in the class dictionary. If it can't be found there, the teacher should supply the correct spelling. Titles can be discussed and selected. Before children write they should have a clear idea of what they are going to tell and how they are going to tell it. The period of preparation is important and should never be omitted.

NATURAL LANGUAGE FOR DEAF CHILDREN

Before going on to other types of composition I would like to state that to my mind it is unnecessary and unwise to teach all the phrases having to do with parts of objects at once. It is true that children who need to use *a piece of* will soon show a need for *a jar of, a tube of, a package of* and many other phrases, but they will not need them all at once. If they have had sufficient practice in using one form there will be little or no trouble with any of the others. These others are learned through conversation, reading and writing in connected language and not in so-called "drills."

To go back to composition! One of the types of composition in this second year should be the writing of very simple notes of thanks, of request, of explanation or of information. A simple note does not require more than two or three sentences. (All notes should be acknowledged!)

Dear Miss ———————,
May we go to the park tomorrow? We want to see the baby elephant. We will be very good.
Your friend (or friends),
Name

Dear Miss ———————,
I am sorry I left my library book at home. I will bring it back next Monday. Is this O.K.? I hope so.
Mary ———————

Dear Mrs. ———————,
One of our turtles died. May we go out to buy another one? Our other turtle is lonesome now.
Your little friend,
Name

Dear Miss ———————,
We had a lovely time in the park. We liked the baby elephant very much. Thank you for our good time.
Love from Class II

In addition to notes, friendly letters should be written. Where children are day students letters can be written to relatives and friends. They should tell something about what the children are doing and should contain news—not just sentences of one kind or another of no interest to the persons receiving them. Hearing children of eight or nine do not write long letters nor should the deaf.

It is never too early to give the deaf child a *feeling* for what is right in a letter. I would not allow a child to write, "You sent me a dress." Instead I would explain that her mother knew that, but didn't know the child had worn it to school that day or didn't know

64

if the children liked it. A child should not write to his father, "You came to see me last Sunday." He should say, "I was happy to see you last Sunday." It is not difficult to train little children to know how to write a satisfactory letter. The child who has been told that his mother is ill should know better than to write, "Dear Mother, You are sick." He might more appropriately write, "I am sorry you are sick. Please get well soon."—or, "I hope you will be all better very soon." One child wrote to his parents, "Thursday was my birthday. I was eight years old." He may have written correct sentences, but he certainly had not the slightest concept of what a letter might be. I always tried to make my own pupils think of letter writing as one way to sit down and talk to a person who was in another place—a friendly conversation on paper.

There are an infinite number of ways in which to get written and spoken everyday language. A picture of a class doll can be put into a little book which would be a collection of "write-ups" on the doll's experiences—getting lost, having a doll party, hiding from the class, going to the hospital, tearing a dress, visiting another class, going to assembly. All these experiences, and many more, would afford opportunities for compositions involving daily language needs.

The writing and speaking of common and individual experiences is a splendid way to develop good compositions, build up an ever-widening vocabulary and gain practical application of language principles learned. Deaf children certainly need much of this kind of work. They also need work that is fanciful, imaginative, entertaining and thought-provoking. The language program should provide for all these needs. The lipreading and reading programs should further supplement the language plan.

I have devoted a great deal of space to composition, for it is the crux of the language teaching in schools for the deaf. Exercises and drills may have their place, but we dwell on these only that they may be used in expressing ideas, thoughts and feelings. That is what composition, oral or written, does.

Language principles taught this year should be those that the children show a need for—those they try to use and do not fully know. The teacher must note these as they crop up in conversation and writing. In a talkative class there will be many things to stress —verb tenses, question forms, prepositions, pronouns, use of *one and the other, some, none, any, somebody, nobody,* the articles *a, an* and *the,* and other language principles. Whatever techniques the teacher uses should have to do with real facts and real situations. The pupils should have each language principle clearly explained, and when it is understood they should be given follow-up exercises to further impress *use* of the principle. There is no way to fix the habit of correctly using language except through actually using it in a meaningful way, so we must have constant repetition. To get this the teacher must provide the right sort of exercises. If an exercise is to benefit the child, it must provide for more than merely filling in a blank with whatever form is desired. It should stimulate the child's thinking, and he should be using the language to express an idea. He should see the connection between the exercise and the use of the particular principle on which he is working. Each exer-cise should be tied up with a life situation—something from the children's experience or observation.

The teacher must know the difference between a constructive exercise and one which is pure rote or memory work with no asso-ciation of ideas, no interest, no vividness of impression. Unless an exercise is constructive, there will be no mental development.

A drill that is not applied to the meaning and use of language is not only useless but harmful. It is possible for a child to get the knack of filling in blanks or writing out forms and yet have a very meager command of language for his everyday use. As an example, the child may be quite adept at doing such an exercise as:

went	saw	buy
did—go	did—see	did—buy

Even so, in his conversation and written work this same child might say, "I did not bought the pencil," or "Mary did not gave me a book." What he needs is understanding, then practice in thinking and writing sentences that require, in this instance, the use of the past negative! No child can memorize all the past negative forms of all the verbs he needs. He will have to have more than memory to fortify himself for future correct usage. He will have to understand the underlying principle. Hence, an explanation should be given, making the problem clear to the learner. There should then be many opportunities for repetition.

It is not unusual for deaf children to have trouble with past negative forms. There is some logic in their use of the past form with *did*. Have they not been told that when a verb tells about something that is "finished" they must use the past tense? Have not these forms been acceptable—*made, saw, went, watched, fed* and many others? What they need is to see how the past negative is formed, not just to be given the form and told to remember it. The child will have to figure out the past negative tense of many verbs —he cannot be given the form for every verb. There are too many.

I have often clarified the formation of the past negative of verbs for deaf children who were acquainted with the tense as it occurred over and over again in everyday use, and yet had difficulty when trying to use new verbs in that tense. I asked them to give me some verbs and then we made a list as follows:

NAME OF VERB	PAST	PAST WITH NOT
go	went	did not go
make	made	did not make
talk	talked	did not talk

We talked about the word *did* and the children agreed that it specified the *past* tense. Therefore when we were using the past negative, *did* made the form signify past action and so we did not need another "past" verb. What did we do? We just used the *name* of the verb. The children caught on at once and with practically no errors gave the past negative forms of many, many verbs—even new ones that were suggested by me. Now they had something to go on! The next step was of course to follow through with meaningful remarks by the pupils: "My mother did not come to see me last week." "I did not go to the movies with my brother." "Miss S——— did not come to school today." "We did not give our show last week." Once there was sufficient repetition of the verb form, we discussed the fact that usually people used contracted forms in conversation, and *didn't* was acceptable and often quite natural.

Elliptical sentences may have their place in tests for content subjects, but as a means for the development of language they have no value in the opinion of this writer. It may be an accomplishment for a child to fill in blanks for *one* and *the other* and do it correctly, but it is not necessarily learning. Sentences like the following are of little interest to a child.

1. John had two pencils.
   ＿＿＿ was red and ＿＿＿ was blue.
2. Mary found two coins.
   ＿＿＿ was a penny and ＿＿＿ was a dime.

How much better to give the child ideas for incorporating this language form into sentences of his own making! Perhaps a question could be used as a starter.

TEACHER: "Mary, how many dresses do you have in your locker?"
MARY: "Two."
TEACHER: "Two! That's nice. Are they new?"
MARY: "One is new and the other is rather old."
TEACHER: "How many dresses do you have upstairs, Jane?"
JANE: "I have two new dresses, too."
TEACHER: "Did your mother make them?"
JANE: "She made *one* and bought *the other.*"

To get variety in the use of this particular principle it is well not to confine its use to differences in color, size and shape. The teacher should ask such questions as: "Where are our tables?" (*One* is in the library and *the other* is in the hall.) "Tell me what your new blouses are made of." (*One* is made of silk and *the other* is made of cotton.) "Where did you get those pencils?" (I found *one* and my mother gave me *the other.*)

One mistake teachers should avoid when trying to get usage of any language principle from their pupils is that of trying to get work from a child when he hasn't first been given enough ideas. No one can draw water from an empty well! The teacher must first fill her pupils with all sorts of suggestions, ideas and knowledge before trying to get back from them something better than uninteresting, trite or empty illustrations of principles of language.

Learning involves understanding and no effort should be spared to ascertain whether the child actually understands the language either given to him or volunteered by him. When he understands the language he must use it, but he should be given time to establish the habit of using correct forms. It has never been expected that one correction should suffice to correct the faulty language of a child with hearing, nor should one correction be considered sufficient for the child who lacks hearing. A friendly reminder will not be amiss: "Don't you remember how I told you to say that yesterday? It was this way." Frequently it will accomplish more direct results than a chiding or an admonition to "sit down and think about it." The wise teacher will do all in her power to keep the deaf child from developing a feeling of insecurity and a sense of inability to master the English language, or from believing that he is inadequate in the use of the language he has been taught.

There is no set way to teach a language principle. One teacher may use one approach and get good results, while another may attack the same problem in an entirely different way and yet secure the same desired results. What matters is the underlying philosophy of teaching language to deaf children. Many a potentially fine teacher has been handicapped by having to teach the principles of language in an unrealistic manner when, if she had been allowed to use her own ideas, she would have done greater service to those she had to teach. Each teacher should have freedom in teaching, though I hasten to add that the basic philosophy of the school should undergird this freedom. There must be continuity in method throughout a school, but this can be maintained while at the same time taking advantage of the individual teacher's talents and abilities.

Language teaching, in every grade, should be an all-day affair for the deaf child just as it is for the hearing child. Granted, we need periods for particular stress on definite constructions or principles, but these periods should not be thought of as the only time in which language is taught. Such periods should not be drawn out to the point at which interest begins to lag. When there is no longer a state of readiness to learn the teacher is wasting her own time as well as that of her pupils. The teacher who stimulates and guides her pupils in all their activities will find that no time is lost through inertia or because of forced attention.

The teacher should know what to expect from each pupil and see that each does the best he can. She may have to give more and greater opportunities to one child and more structured material to another in order to meet their needs. Each and every deaf child is an individual with his own capacity for learning, even though he may be one with his group in the many activities and happenings of the school day. The teacher must not only follow the admonition to "know thyself" but must also know her pupils.

Seven- and eight-year-olds are fun to know, a joy to be with, a satisfaction to the teacher. For them each day is a delight, for the teacher each day is a joy and a challenge. The teacher must be both a follower and a leader, a close friend and a guide. The opportunities given to her to enrich the lives of the children entrusted to her care are, in actuality, great gifts. Like all precious gifts these opportunities must be both used and treasured.

CHAPTER VI

ESTABLISHING PATTERNS OF SELF-EXPRESSION

Knowledge and timber shouldn't be much used till they are seasoned.

OLIVER WENDELL HOLMES
Autocrat of the Breakfast Table

TEACHERS of the deaf are continually asking how they can get better and more lasting results from their teaching of language. They want to know how they can improve, what they do that is wrong, why they have such meager success. The perfect answers probably never will materialize, but searching for them will help the teacher to explore and find new and better ways of teaching language. The teacher who is aware of a need for improving her techniques is well on the way toward the accomplishment of greater achievement on the part of her pupils.

The core of the problems we face in our work with the deaf is in our need for a re-evaluation of our methods of teaching. Before a change can come, however, there must develop in all educators of the deaf a consciousness of the need for the change. A great and encompassing awakening of this consciousness, on the part of teachers of the deaf, would prove a great blessing to our deaf children. It would provide an abundance of teaching methods and techniques that would solve many of the ever-present problems having to do with the teaching of the language arts to the deaf. All of us who love the deaf child, and who have his interests at heart, look forward longingly to the day when we shall reach new horizons that signify, for him, a happy and rightful heritage.

The teacher of the deaf must be resourceful. She will have to find many opportunities for creating normal and natural circumstances calling for the language response she desires. Real benefit will be obtained by the child only from his use of language *in situations that are analogous to those he will meet in real life.* This sort of teaching requires alertness and inventiveness on the part of the teacher and a constant awareness of the fact that no hearing child, much less a *deaf* one, can be taught language by means of unassociated and meaningless use of words and monotonous unrelated drill sentences.

It is not difficult to interest deaf boys and girls if one is bound heart and soul in the undertaking. Children are quick to sense genuineness of interest and respond to it. All deaf children like to learn and like to work when the atmosphere of the classroom *and* the school is conducive to learning. From my own experience as a teacher I am convinced that deaf children of all ages want to learn, appreciate what has been taught to them and are happy over their own achievements. As the teacher weaves newly-taught language into her conversation, reading, speech lesson, lipreading, arithmetic, social studies and whatever other subjects the class may be studying, her pupils will see for themselves the value of that language, not as a form of subject matter so much as a very useful and much needed and desired tool. Having a command of language is not only a necessity to the deaf child in his daily contact with hearing people, it is the open door to happy, satisfying, broadening and rewarding living.

Let us consider for a moment the language needs of the deaf child of nine or ten years of age. If he attended the school nurseries he has been in school seven years—the first three years being in the preschool where he learned mostly through play activities but where he absorbed an understanding of language through lipreading and, in some cases, acoustical training. During the past three or four years he has learned some of the fundamentals of English. He can express himself in complete sentences when they are called for; he can make correct use of many question forms; he has a lipreading vocabulary of several hundred words. He is interested in books suitable to his age, but needs help in reading them. He is ready to branch out in his use of language and, if he has been well taught, should cover a considerable amount of ground at this time. The child by now should be ready to learn to express himself not only correctly but interestingly as well.

It seems unfortunate that in many cases so much time and energy have been expended on the construction of sentences that are just grammatically correct, that little time has been left for concentration on the writing of sentences for beauty and symmetry or for the entertainment afforded by fresh and vivid expression. The determination to get correct sentences has overshadowed the realization that grammatically correct sentences can also be interesting, entertaining and beautiful. Too often the teacher who has struggled desperately to do away with blatant errors has learned to accept a sentence thankfully if it is correct, even though the thought is not couched in phrases naturally used by the hearing. I have often been surprised at the rapidity with which a young teacher will come to accept the odd expressions employed by her deaf pupils, often unconsciously annexing these expressions to her own vocabulary. Fortunate is the teacher with someone (probably a young, uninhibited relative) who checks up on her by asking, "Why do you say 'letter paper' for 'writing paper'?" "Does a deaf child have to say 'slate' all the time? Can't he ever say 'blackboard'?" "People don't say 'How much does that cost?' They say, 'How much is it?'" Having had several nieces and nephews, I know what correcting rods hearing children can be.

We certainly want our deaf children to use good language, but we also desire that they should comprehend and appreciate good language when they see it. We should not wait until they are in the upper school to give them insight into the art of speaking and writing. Johnny doesn't have to wait until he gets into the middle school to learn that he can change the sentence, "Miss A ran into the room because she was late," to "Miss A rushed into the room because she was late." And Mary, when very young, may learn to write, "Nancy has a sunny smile," or to describe some other classmate by telling of some outstanding characteristic, as "Jack is always happy." What I wrote long years ago still holds true. The "yellow hair, blue eyes and rosy cheek" method of description is actually a waste of time. It is not even a good way to get practice in the use of the verbs *to have* and *to be,* and serves no good purpose whatever. Such bits of language have no future use as far as the child is concerned.

Nine-year-olds can learn that simple sentences can be varied by the use of different adjectives or verbs. They can learn to discriminate in choosing words to express themselves. To develop the habit of discrimination, one plan might be to let each child in the class contribute one descriptive sentence about a child or an object. Make a list of the sentences and have the *pupils* select the most telling one. It will not be difficult for the teacher to make the

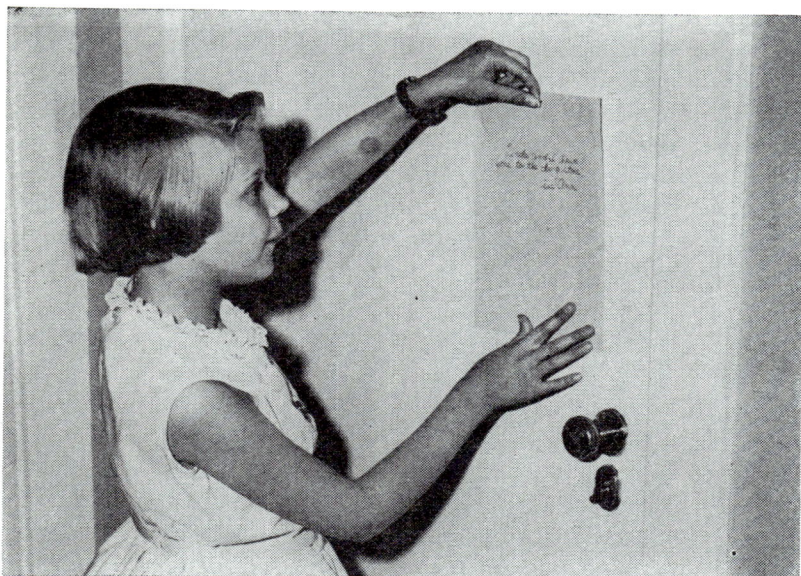

Using language at home.

children understand that giving the color of the eyes and hair does not tell much about a person, since many people have the same coloring, but that a glimpse of that person's habits or mannerisms through differentiating expressions will give a better mental picture of him. Examples of this are: "Her hair is always ruffled." "Her eyes twinkle." "Her eyes are merry." These are individual descriptions and the children can eventually be made to feel this.

Children at the age of nine and ten are, like their hearing brothers and sisters, given to fancy and inventiveness in play. They like to be busy and to talk about their busy-ness. Hearing children do not talk much about going for a walk (unless it be an unusual one) or taking a bath, or going to bed or to school or to church. They talk about their play, their toys and other possessions, their imaginings, the things they see, want, do and use.

By this time the *daily* news period should be discontinued and perhaps just week-end news covered. There are too many other ways of working on connected language and putting emphasis on self-expression. The conversation period will take care of regular news. The children should not strive solely for correct language. They should aim for, and recognize, an interesting way of putting their thoughts on paper. They should see that one interesting short paragraph is worth ten long ones, no matter how correct, which

73

have been written without having been thought out. If the children realize that they can make their paragraphs bring a smile or a look of pleasure, they will endeavor to find words that make "good pictures" instead of concentrating all their effort on remembering sentences in the expectation of having a perfect paper.

One way in which the group can be started on the way to discrimination might be for the teacher to put little paragraphs about one thing or another on the blackboard, and allow the children to choose the one they prefer. For example:

I

John has a dog. It is big and black. It is at home. It barks at people. They are afraid. They run away.

II

John has a big, black dog at home. Sometimes it growls at people and frightens them. Maybe they think it is a bear.

A discussion as to why one paragraph is more interesting than the other will help the children to *feel* the difference between a collection of choppy statements and a smooth running group of sentences. They cannot put this feeling into words but it is there. If this practice is continued it will bear fruit.

Children are generally delighted to learn a new descriptive word. They can appreciate the fact that it is more interesting to describe Mary as a "sleepyhead" than to say she "is sleepy every day." They enjoy thinking of "picture words" for their stories and other types of composition. Learning to assemble their thoughts, and deciding on words to be used when they write, gives them confidence in what they are doing. Confidence begets pleasure. In all that the children do in written language, the first consideration should be given to the quality of the writing—no matter how simple a piece has been written. After that has been done an analysis of errors should be made. The results are always better if, for instance, the teacher tells Sharon that she wrote a cute story and chose good words, and only after that adds, "But your verb is wrong, can you correct it?" or, "You left out a very important little word. Read this again and see if you can remember the little word you forgot." Deaf children throughout all the grades should be familiar with such procedure and should manifest a personal interest in all their compositions and in criticism of them.

As a preliminary to writing little stories a teacher might try having the children tell in one or two sentences why they like a thing or a person. They will have a more picturesque vocabulary and an awareness of the value of words if they become familiar with such responses as: "I like John because he is always good-natured." "I like Mary because she's so clean and neat." "Jack is never cross. I think he likes everybody."

Telling about people in pictures is also a good way to build a worthwhile vocabulary.

> TEACHER: "Tell me what you think about this picture, Laurie."
> LAURIE: "The man is old. He looks funny because he's wearing old-fashioned clothes."
> TEACHER: "How about this boy, Tommy?"
> TOMMY: "His clothes are old and torn. He looks poor and I think he's very cold."

Writing about a favorite toy or possession is also helpful—"I like my big doll. She has lovely long hair." "I like my new book. It has beautiful pictures in it." "I love my Teddy. He is old and he has only one eye. My daddy gave him to me a long time ago." "My truck is strong, I can put heavy rocks in it."

Making up stories about a child who was naughty and telling what the child did—or a story about a little girl or a pet—will also be of interest and help to the children.

Toy stories should be continued, as children love them. Nine- and ten-year-olds can tell very fascinating little tales about the objects they are using.

Learning to follow simple outlines is a great advantage to the deaf child. The simplest form would be:

Where did you go?
What did you see?
How did you like it?

Later that form should be changed to:

Tell: Where you went:
What you saw:
How you liked it:
or
Tell: What you made:
What it is like:
What you will do with it:

The use of outlines, whether oral or written, will help the child to organize his thoughts and make him stick to the point in writing his compositions.

The teacher should constantly bear in mind the fact that ideas form the basis of language expression. She must stimulate the child's ideas, give him quantities of new impressions through conversations about his experiences, happenings of concern or interest to him, stories, newspaper items, planned activities and selected reading. She has to see to it that the pupils have things to think about, talk about and write about.

As the teacher fosters ideas she must also fortify the children with a vocabulary that is comprehensive enough to put the ideas into writing. Much work must be done on vocabulary building. However, it is well for the teacher to remember constantly that it is of little use to teach new words simply in order to enlarge the vocabulary. It is also futile to introduce and teach new language principles without relation to need of expression. The child must have both vocabulary and principles so that he may be equipped to express himself.

It is my conviction that words or principles, taught in a regular order as given in a term's outline, probably will not be used spontaneously. But words and language forms learned in natural association, in connection with an activity or experience and necessary for expressing what a child has done, will be remembered and will become a permanent part of that child's language and will be used whenever the setting calls for their use. It therefore goes without saying that all new words and language should first be used in the situations which naturally call for them. They make more lasting impressions because of their association with the activity or situation. When a new word, verb tense or language construction is necessary in order to express exactly what the child is trying to say, the teacher should give it to him. If a child says, "I saw a woman on the street. She wheeled a baby in a carriage," he should be given the form *was wheeling* right then and there, with a simple explanation. If he says, "I went home Friday. My family moved to a new house," he should be given *had moved* with the explanation that the moving took place before he went home. I do not intend to convey the impression that the matter of the past perfect tense should be gone into in detail at this time, but I do think that incorrect uses should not be allowed to pass. Sometimes it is the teacher's fault that deaf children have stilted and queer language.

Whenever a child uses some recently learned language principle, or some new word or words, the matter should be commented upon and the child should be praised for his initiative. If this is done effectively it will be an inducement to the other pupils to apply what they have learned. If a child wrote only two or three sentences, but what he wrote was unusual—or surprising—or very interesting, the teacher should make a point of this and praise it accordingly.

Returning to various uses of language, let me emphasize that there should be many notes written and delivered. These could include notes asking if the class may take a trip and giving the reasons —requests to go to the homemaking department to make a cake or to have a party—requests to go to the library to get new reading table books or to change readers—notes asking to have window shades fixed, pictures hung, new panes of glass put in (these to the house director)—notes of thanks for work done, for privileges granted, for requests allowed, for new schoolroom materials—notes of apology for being late, for accidents in the classroom or playroom, for lost library books—the possibilities are endless.

These notes should be short and informal. They should be answered, either in writing or orally. Children usually enjoy writing notes, and it is an excellent way to make practical use of language that has been taught. In one week at school I received notes from a second-year class asking me to come to see a house they had made, from another class asking me to please come to see their arithmetic work, from a third-year class asking if they could go out on a trip, from a fourth-year class thanking me for permitting them to go to the museum and telling me about the trip.

Making booklets about a boy or a girl or a pet or a doll, and adding a short story each week, will provide occasions for the use of language and will at the same time provide review. To give just one illustration let us assume that one child, Bruce, wants to make a book about a boy named Jack. He may title the book just "Jack," or he may prefer "My Book about Jack." He will cut out a picture of a boy for a frontispiece. His first story would be an introduction to Jack, telling his age, where he lives (in city or country), and other facts that will place Jack for future readers. Then from time to time there will be short accounts about what Jack can do, what he likes to do, what he does with his friends or his family. There will be stories perhaps of trips, surprises, accidents, good times. When the books are in progress other children should be allowed to read them and discuss them. When the books are completed each child should take his booklet home. Such books may be illustrated by the children.

Books about dolls afford many opportunities for the writing of compositions. Dolls can become lost, or can hide, or can go to parties, be sick and need a doctor, receive new clothes, go visiting another doll, be naughty, be very good and, in fact, go through many of the same experiences as do the little writers of these stories.

Writing "pretend" stories is another form of composition and most children like to pretend either that they are people (fireman, policeman, nurse) or things (the clock, the window pole, the blackboard). Examples of stories by children follow:

I am the bell. The children go to recess, or to lunch when I ring. They are glad that I am in school.

I am the wastepaper basket. The children throw old papers into me. I keep the room neat.

I'm the window pole. When it is warm I open the window so the children can have fresh air. When it is cold I shut the window so they will be warm. I am very useful.

Sometimes these stories can be very revealing. One child, who longed always to be very important and who desperately needed someone to look up to her and give her special attention, chose to be the big clock in the main office. This clock was always supposed to show the correct time and teachers and pupils often referred to it. So this particular child wrote:

I am the big clock in the office. I am always right. People look at me because they want to know the right time. I am glad that I am this clock.

Sometimes writing compositions that begin "When I was little," or "When I am grown up," will give the children a chance to use their language in a personal way.

A class storybook will allow for the use of individual compositions. This can be made from a large scrapbook. When a child writes a particularly good story it can be pasted in this book. Its title can be added to the table of contents. Such a class book will make for good reading for the whole class and provide for repeated reading of meaningful language.

Through the morning conversation period, which by now should be less one-sided than in the early grades, the teacher can discover the needs of the children for certain language principles, incidental expressions and definite additions to their vocabularies.

One of the biggest problems for the teacher will now be to help the children ask questions correctly. They will have many to ask and will need to know how to form the various types of questions. The office of a question is to obtain information or to satisfy one's curiosity. The only exception to this would be the questions asked on a test. Therefore it would seem that the best way to teach the various question forms would be through *use*—first *use* by the teacher and then *use* by the child. I think it helpful for the teacher to ask questions orally in connection with all phases of classroom work and in every possible situation. The forms are difficult and it is easier for the child to understand a question than to ask one.

Seeing the question in use for some time before working on it is a good thing. It acquaints the child with the form before he must struggle with it himself.

Since the legitimate use of a question is to satisfy curiosity or to get information, the teacher should be sure that that is the way questions are used. Having children formulate questions from given answers is unnatural and in no way connected with real life, and this form of drill should be avoided. A question form can always be taught in connection with a natural circumstance. Having children work on such questions as *by whom? in whose? from whom?* should not be given at this time. It would be most unnatural to say, "By whom was the book given to you?" rather than "Who gave you the book?"—"In whose desk are the crayons?" rather than "Where are the crayons?" or "Who has the crayons?"

Asking questions in a guessing contest will provide repetition in use of questions. This activity was explained in the chapters on preschool and the first year of the lower school so I will not go into detail here. Using the same questions frequently, under differing circumstances, will give children ease in asking questions in general. Children must have sufficient practice if they are going to use correct forms spontaneously when they want to know something.

Playing games on occasion will offer opportunities for using questions. Ask one child to go out of the classroom for a minute or two. When he has returned have the other children ask him questions to see if they can discover where he went or what he saw or did. This is fun if not overdone. The children could ask such questions as: "Did you talk to anyone?" (No)—"Did you get a drink?" (No)—"Did you go to the library?" (No) To make it more like a game the children can be taught the expressions "Am I warm?" or "I give up." The child who guesses what was done could then go out of the room.

It is difficult to find written exercises on question forms that are natural in their use. For instance, the teacher will not be richly rewarded if she writes on the board, "I went away for the week end," and asks the class to write five questions about this. The child may write: "Who went away for the week end?" "When did you go away for the week end?" He will be concerned only with writing questions and will not be interested in the teacher's trip. Furthermore, he may produce the correct language, but it will have no importance whatever for him.

The same situation could be used by the teacher *orally*. Her conversation could possibly run like this:

TEACHER: "Oh, I had such a marvelous time over the week end."
CLASS: "What did you do?"
TEACHER: "I went to the country."
CLASS: "Did you go to a farm?"
TEACHER: "No, I just visited a friend who lives in the country. She has a beautiful garden.
CLASS: "Did she give you any flowers?"
TEACHER: "Yes, indeed. She gave me a big box of flowers. I picked them myself."
CLASS: "May we see them?"
TEACHER: "Yes, and you may pick out the ones you like for our room."
HARRY: "What else did you do in the country?"
TEACHER: "I walked through a beautiful woods. It was very still in there."
FRED: "Were there any animals in the woods?"
TEACHER: "Only rabbits. There were birds, too."

What a difference there is between the first written questions and the latter oral questions!

Again, a poor way to teach question forms is for the teacher to say, "I saw something pretty in Bloomingdale's window last night. Ask me five questions." Suppose a child writes, "Did you see a beautiful dress?" and that is what she did see. If he has to think up four more questions before he can turn in his paper he will be hard put to it to write something which makes sense to him.

An ingenious teacher will be able to stimulate the children to ask questions. Having planned a neighborhood trip in her mind, she might tell the children when they come to the classroom to go and get their hats and coats. The first question would no doubt be "Why?" When told they were going out, other questions should naturally follow such as: "Where are we going?" "Why are we going there?" "When will we come back?" "What will we see there?"

There are countless occasions each day when questions can and should be asked by the children. Some of these will be simple. Some will take a lot of teaching and practice. Much repetition is needed for such questions as: "How far are we going?" "How long will it take?" Since this is so I think such question forms as "What is——— for?" should be given to the children when they are curious about some new gadget that has come their way, but there should be no drill on this form at all. We ourselves ask "What's it for?" only when we are seeking enlightenment. The little children at Lexington often ask "What for?" when taken out of class for some reason or other. Where they picked this up no one knows, but they know where to apply it.

Another question form that I would have children use only incidentally would be "What is ——— made of?" In a guessing game this is a handy question but it does not require formalized drill. If the question "What kind of___?" is taught it should be answered not only by adjectives (strong, big, good, pretty, red), but also by nouns—"What kind of flower is it?" "*A daisy.*" "What kind of bird did you see?" "*A robin.*"

Why questions require more than one type of reply, and the responses should be taken up one at a time.

Why are you crying? I hurt myself, *or* Mother went home.
Why are you yawning? I'm tired.
Why did you go upstairs? To comb my hair.
Why did you leave the room? To get a drink.
Why did Mary go to the hospital? Because she was sick.

One final word about the use of questions. It is necessary to get continuous meaningful practice in using the forms needed in the daily round of classroom and playroom affairs. If the children are to acquire the habit of asking these questions correctly, they should not have new forms thrust at them too rapidly or before they are ready for them.

Question forms are not the only language principles with which deaf children have difficulty. There are unending language forms to be learned if our pupils in schools for the deaf are to be able to use habitually the correct expression for each and every need.

Most children, by the time they have been in the regular classes beyond preschool for a few years, demonstrate a need for new sentence forms. One of these is that in which we have the subject inverted. (Example: There are some books in the closet.) All sentence forms should be introduced and used informally by the teacher in conversation and reading before any definite work is given on them. A child may say, "Three new books are on your desk." Even though I had not taught the new sentence form, I would give it to him then and there and have him say, "There are three new books on your desk."

When the children evince a need for the form, more direct teaching should be undertaken. Perhaps its use in directions might make a good beginning. A teacher could place things about, for example, and say:

There is an apple in the closet. It's for you, Jane.
There is a banana on the bottom shelf. That's for Mary.
There is a surprise for each of you in your desk drawer.

The teacher might also have a child take a peek into some other teacher's room and on her return tell what that teacher had on her desk.

> There is a green blotter on Miss B's desk. There is a vase of flowers, too.
> What is on her window sill? There is a plant on it.
> Was it there yesterday? No.
> What was there yesterday?

Incidental questions used during the day could be:

> Mary, is there anything on the top shelf of the closet? Yes, there is.
> What's there?
> Who put it there?
> > or
> There is someone at the door. Will you open the door, Patty?
> There are no children in the yard. Where are they?

Talking about pictures can provide repetition in the use of these types of sentences:

> Is there a baby in your picture, Joan?
> No. There is a woman.
> Is there a dog in your picture, Margie?
> Yes, there is. He's cute.
> Are there any other animals?
> There's a cat.

There is one thing the teacher should be very careful not to do, and that is to give an exercise like this:

> Write these sentences another way and use "There is _____."
> 1. Some paste is in the closet.
>   There is some paste in the closet.
> 2. A tree is in the yard.
>   There is a tree in the yard.

Such an exercise will make the child think that the sentences are both correct and are interchangeable. But they are not. The sentence, "Some paste is in the closet," is stilted, unnatural and awkward. It is also very poor English.

Why do deaf children make so many errors in their use of English? The main reason, of course, is that they are deaf and have had to learn English the hard way. Sometimes, though, this typical "deaf language" is due to faulty presentation and teaching. The child who writes "a box of a dress" or "a box of a hat" has not had it made clear to him that some things are sold in boxes (are boxed), such as a box of saltines, or a box of writing paper, while other things are just put in boxes for easy handling. Again the child who thinks "a pair of" means *two articles*—two things thrown together—does not have a true concept of that phrase. "A pair of" means two *like* things. If there is to be a pair of red gloves, for example, one must be for the left hand and one for the right hand, and both must be the same size. If these facts are not so, the child has two red gloves but not a pair of red gloves.

Teachers of the deaf have great responsibility in guiding their pupils through the intricacies of the English language, and each step of the way must be clear and straight to the child.

Children who were properly taught the meaning and use of *one and the other* should not have trouble with phrases like *one and the others* or *one, another and the others*. If they understood *some* and *any* and when to use them, they should adapt easily to the use of *somebody* and *anybody* or *something* and *anything*. All too often the teacher presents a few illustrations of the language principle she thinks she is teaching, and has the child give further similar examples. Yet the child isn't clear in his mind about the language but is merely remembering it. He will eventually reach a place where he can't just "remember" but will have to *think* a thing out for himself. All teaching of the deaf should prepare each child for that time when he can learn new language for himself by making associations with what was previously taught him.

New verbs and new tenses are always coming up in every class throughout the school. Misuse of verbs is probably the cause of fifty percent of the errors made in the use of English by deaf pupils and deaf adults. The only way to overcome this common fault is to see that verbs are used by the children in connected language at all times. In the age group of which we are now talking, there is still no need for the children to know every single tense of every new verb that comes up. They need repeated use of the verb in those tenses which occur continually in all they want to say or write. There will be verbs the children will need in the present or past progressive and probably, to a limited degree, in the present perfect. There will be much work needed on the past negative and past interrogative of some verbs, but not every verb the children happen to know. They should not have to conjugate verbs in every tense.

The deaf child *needs* to know that when he is speaking of another person (Tom, Jane, he, she), of an object (the cup, it), he must use the third person and *always* do so. If this is clear to him he will learn to use correct forms through his understanding of the underlying principles of the constructions of verb tenses and the agreement of subject noun and predicate verb. Let us take, for example, nine-year-old David. David knows he must say, "Mary *plays* with my sister every afternoon." He understands why this is correct. He should then be able to write: "She *talks* to my father when he comes home. She likes to come to my house." David, when he has learned that when speaking of himself or others he must use *was,* and when he is addressing a person he must use *were,* should not have difficulty when he needs the past progressive forms—*was* reading, *were* writing. When he has learned the difference between singular and plural forms (and learned them not through definition but through application) he should be able to apply his knowledge to new situations and not continue to guess and to make such errors as he *have* or the boys *has.* Teachers who insist that deaf children *think* before they speak or write, do these children a great service. The deaf, just as everyone else, must learn to apply new knowledge to that already acquired.

True, much teaching and much work on the part of pupils has to be done on verbs. The teacher should take her cue on what verbs to stress from the conversations, questionings and written work of her pupils. When they are ready for the verb *to ask* or *to tell* she will know it. When they need the present perfect tense she will discover that, too. Children who are accustomed to talking a great deal and to putting their thoughts, feelings and ideas on paper will have to have the ability to use verbs in many forms. They will need to add to their list of verbs continually. Teachers would do well to stay away from cut-and-dried activities in teaching verbs. I do not think the present progressive tense, for example, should be introduced or taught by having a child run around the room, skip, hop or perform any other action. It is much better to introduce this tense in a natural way—"Don't bother Jean. She *is studying.*" "Don't talk to Susie when she *is writing.*" "What *are* the children *doing* in the yard?" "They *are playing* basketball," or "They *are building* a house." From this use of the present progressive tense the children can make more normal application to other things that are going on about them and to discussions about what is taking place in newspaper, magazine and other pictures.

In the classes that we are talking about the children will be adding greatly to their general vocabulary. Many new nouns, adjectives, adverbs, prepositions, interjections and pronouns will be needed to take care of the expanding use of language. Which prepositions? The ones most called for. Which nouns? The ones the children must have if they are to tell about themselves, their relationships with others, their individual and group activities.

In addition to this sort of vocabulary the teacher should watch for opportunities to teach idiomatic expressions and such useful phrases as *big enough, tall enough* (I'm not *tall enough* to reach the top shelf.) , *much too heavy* and *too heavy for me.*

Deaf children need more than the bare facts of language. They need colorful, colloquial, idiomatic language suitable to their age —the kind of language hearing children pick up so easily. To provide this, such language usage should begin in the early grades. There are times when the exclamation "Goody!" is more appropriate than a formal, "I like that." Deaf children need language *also* as an outlet for sudden joy, unexpected surprises, deep feelings and just plain fun. They should have this language. Let us always remember that our *pupils* are also *children.*

CHAPTER VII

IMAGINATION ENRICHES EXPRESSION

A word is dead
When it is said
  Some say.
I say it just
Begins to live
  That day.

EMILY DICKINSON
Life

BEFORE going deeper into this discussion of language I would like to say that my experience has convinced me that language *can* be taught to the deaf in a *natural* manner. There may be those who will disagree with me on first consideration. After careful contemplation of the way in which hearing children acquire language, and after a searching study of the psychology of learning and of the application of this science to the teaching of language to the deaf, I feel sure that many will come to an acknowledgment of the truth of this belief. By *natural* manner I do not mean that the deaf child's language can grow up like Topsy, without care and attention. The natural method is not hit-and-miss. It is not an easy method, or a method without rhyme or reason. To my mind, it requires much more thought and consideration on the part of the teacher than any other method I have yet seen.

To teach in this way the teacher must know not only her subject but also her children—*all* children. She must know what the children are like, how best they will learn, what things will really reach them and take hold. It is only through such knowledge that she can plan her program, take advantage of every opportunity that crops up during the school day and use it as a basis for her teaching of language. She will have to train her mind to take in and to retain all the individual as well as group needs in the language growth of her pupils, to remember each child's weaknesses and to give the kind of help that will eliminate them. No opportunity to strengthen a child's use of language should ever be lost; no indication of a need or desire for new language should ever go unheeded.

It cannot be repeated too often that the teaching of language is an all-day affair, and I do not mean merely a school day of five hours duration. There are many times and many places where the deaf child can and should be learning to use more correct language. I am not referring to a formal language period, but rather to language usage in the halls, dining room, playground, playrooms, infirmary, library, gymnasium and any other place where children congregate. If the teacher is present in any of these areas she should see that the children have the correct language to express what they are thinking or doing. If this language needs more intensive work, it should be taken up in detail when the class is in the schoolroom.

Even counselors or housemothers, who are not trained as teachers, can help their charges to use better language. Many of them do. I was delighted one late afternoon to overhear one of Lexington's counselors saying to one of the primary children, "Why do you say 'want, want' all the time? Can't you say, 'I'd like to'?" That counselor was teaching language in the finest way. On another occasion, in another playroom, I heard a counselor say to a child, "Ask me that in a good question and I'll give you a good answer." Children who are talked to in school, out of school, at home or "abroad" will inevitably have more language and will think of it as a necessity in all human relationships. The deaf child needs not just one teacher but many teachers. His classroom teacher may be his mainstay in his acquisition of language, but what she teaches must be reinforced by others—his parents and school counselors, his teachers of art, gym, eurythmics, crafts and cooking. In fact, he needs the help of all those who are concerned in any way with his daily life, for from all these contributors he should eventually have a language to live by.

Every teacher of the deaf needs to see her children as they are *and* as they will be in five, ten or twenty years. She must never forget that it is the mastery of language in all its forms—spoken, written and comprehended—that gives to the deaf person his ability to live happily and successfully with hearing people who use language as their principal means of communication. It is this lack of use and comprehension of language that sets the deaf person apart from his contemporaries. Without a natural and spontaneous use of language he will be considered different and all too often be grossly misunderstood and greatly underestimated. The deaf need the language of the hearing, not language that is different—watered down, limited, stilted, queer. The conscientious, interested, well-qualified and happy teacher will seek to do her share toward the development of a happy, useful, well-ordered adult life for each and every child who comes under her care.

By the time deaf children are ten or eleven years of age they usually enter the Middle School, or, as sometimes designated, the Intermediate Department. If these pupils are of average mentality, and have been given a good background in the use of language, they should be applying this knowledge in their oral and written work and should be reading with greater ease and efficiency. The use of English should be habitual to them, and they should be ready to increase their command of it and broaden their application of it to whatever they are learning.

Although I say the use of English is, or should be, *habitual,* I do not assume that it will be used correctly in every instance. There will be need for constant teaching and correction. The children will have more and more things to talk about, their range of interests will be widening and their need for an expanding vocabulary will be urgent. At this level children become interested in their community and in the world about them and are developing more abstract concepts and relationships. They are gathering impressions and ideas vicariously. Their vocabulary must cover the language needs of everyday occurrences in addition to the language of the imagination, for children love fanciful tales and like to invent their own stories about persons, animals, places and happenings.

The written work of this group should include many, many original stories. These can be collected and eventually gathered into a pupil-made "book" to be taken home for the edification and entertainment of the family. Having a "Table of Contents" adds interest to such books, as does an attractive cover with the title displayed in some artistic design. I have before me several such books, all of which contain individual stories. The children who wrote these tales were eleven by the end of the school year or during the summer vacation.

One book is called, "My Imaginary Stories." The titles of some of the stories are:

The Deer in the Woods
A Funny Story
A Complication
Snowman Party
A Valentine Contest
A Surprise Visit
Mischief
Teacher of the Deaf
Lost and Found

One of the stories follows:

THE DEER IN THE WOODS

Mr. and Mrs. Deer had four fawns. Their name were Linda, Jack, Sharon and Bobby. One day the fawns went to the forest to play hide-and-seek. Sharon was it. The others ran and hid behind the trees. Sharon looked and looked for them, but she couldn't find them. She jumped to conclusions. She told a friend that they were lost. The friend told another friend and that friend told another friend. They looked and looked for the fawns. They couldn't find them. Sharon was worried and anxious about them. It began to get dark, so she went home. She told her mother that the fawns were lost. Mother said, "Don't be so silly. They are right here. This will teach you a lesson, not to jump to conclusions." Sharon was embarrassed.

Another book is called, "Beverly's Stories." Its table of contents and one complete story follow:

The Freckle Contest
The Quadruplets
Poor Little Snowmanland
The Boy Who Had No Heart
To Hollywood
Kenny and Pal
The Pigeons
Sleeping in the Attic
Owner of a Store
Sherry and the Mouse

THE PIGEONS

Jane woke up one morning and ran to the window. She saw that it was a beautiful day. Jane asked her mother if she could go to Central Park and her mother said, "Yes." When she got there, she fed some pigeons. She saw one pigeon walking alone. She thought it was sick, so she went over to see what had happened. She was very surprise when she saw the pigeon had six little pigeons.

A third book is called simply, "My Imagination." Its stories run like this:

A Dog
A Broken Ladder

Happy, the Snowman
Sparky, the Firedog
Dressing Up
A Baby Chicken
When I Grow Up

A BROKEN LADDER

One day a man came to the neighborhood to put a poster up. He got his ladder from the truck. He went up on the ladder. He had a can of paste with him. He put it on the shelf of the ladder. Then he pasted the poster up. A man was walking by. The shelf broke off. The paste fell on the man's head. He looked like taffy. He felt upset.

Other titles in some of these books were:

In the Woods
A Surprise
The Sorrowful Snowmen
Meeting the President
Shut-Ins
A Librarian
Dancing Car
The Amusement Park
Luke and His Friend

A LIBRARIAN

In the future my ambition is to be a librarian because I love to read books. I will have to go to college for four years. I will have to learn how to file books. I have to know what kind of books young and older children like.

I think being a librarian will be an interesting job.

A very popular set of stories was entitled "Christmas in Many Lands." There were ten "chapters," each telling how Christmas is celebrated in another country. This project required research in the library. It ended by an assembly presentation of the way Christmas is observed in other lands, the costumes and props of which were made by the children with the help of the art teacher.

Another book made by each child was about an imaginary family. The children thought up names for their families and then decided on the titles for their books. Some of the titles suggested were:

At Home with the Smiths
The Kaye Family
Fun with the Whites
The Gordons at Home

A representative chapter follows:

AN AIRPLANE TRIP

(From a book called, "Fun with the Whites")
One Saturday after Jean's birthday Jean, Penelope and Frank got a letter from Aunt Roz and Uncle Lou. They invited them

to come to Salt Lake City for the summer. Jean jumped up and down until she was out of breath. Mother heard Jean jump up and down so she went outside and asked her why she was so excited. Jean showed Mother the letter. Mother said to Jean, "How nice! You must write a thank-you note to Aunt Roz and Uncle Lou."

On June tenth Jean and Frank's school closed. Then in the afternoon they packed their trunks. They were very excited.

The next morning Jean and Frank woke up with the birds. Their parents were already up. They hurried to get dressed. After breakfast Daddy told Jean and Frank that they were going by airplane. They were excited because they had never flown.

About nine o'clock Daddy drove the family to La Guardia Airport. On the way Jean asked Daddy at what time she and Frank would reach Salt Lake City. He said that they would be there about seven o'clock. When the family reached La Guardia Airport, Father asked the attendant where Flight 31 was. He told Father that Flight 31 was at Gate one hundred seven. Then the family went there. When they reached the gate, Father told the children that he was going with them. They were very glad to hear that.

Then it was time for Father and the children to take off. They climbed aboard. The door was closed. The propellers started turning and away they went.

The first story in each book was an introduction to the family, telling how many people were in it, where they lived, what pets they had, and giving other pertinent information.

From time to time various stories were added. They told of family picnics, surprises, trips, illnesses, birthday celebrations, school events. Each book was entirely individual. Although each child, for instance, wrote about a family outing, the stories were slanted toward the particular family of the child writing. There was a basic vocabulary as the class worked out expressions and good descriptive words—all agog, could hardly wait, full of excitement, up bright and early, up with the birds, delightful, a perfect day.

Not all hearing people write equally well. Ability varies. One person can sit down and write a very interesting, informative and entertaining letter while another person can write no more than the bare essentials and not do even this well. Nor do the deaf all write with the same degree of skill. Teachers should make allowances for individual differences in the use of language. The child with a gift for writing should be inspired and encouraged to produce the best that is in him. The child with less skill and imagination should also receive much help, but he should not be compared unfavorably to his more gifted classmates. He can write shorter and simpler compositions and be helped by being given some good descriptive words to add to what he has said. He, too, should be able to take pride in his work.

Before any compositions are written there must be genuine preparation. Ideas must be discussed, new vocabulary taught, words and expressions with similar meanings discussed and a decision made as to which word more nearly suits the idea to be conveyed. This preparation may go on for two or three days. A child does not learn to express himself correctly and interestingly by writing a journal or a composition every day in the week. He must be taught how to write well—how to express himself interestingly, both orally and in writing.

When the ideas for a story have been decided upon and a title chosen, then there should be work on good beginning sentences. If all the pupils are writing on the same subject, a number of good beginning sentences can be put on the blackboard and the children can discuss them—"Does this opening sentence make me want to read the rest of the story? Does it make me curious? Does it tell too much?" Let us take as an example a composition about "John and His Dog." Children can be taught to see the difference between a beginning such as, "John has a funny black and white dog," and "John has a dog that makes everyone laugh," or "John's dog does some very funny tricks." Usually children, with little or no prodding, become very particular about how they commence a story. There is all the difference in the world as to a *feeling* for language between the child who starts a composition on "The New Dress" with the sentence, "Mary got paint on her new dress," and "An awful thing happened to Mary when she wore her new dress for the first time." In teaching a class of eleven-year-olds, I once spent three weeks on a composition. The first week we all worked on good beginnings and good endings, the second week on writing the body of the composition, and the third week on polishing the language. During this time the children learned not only new vocabulary, new idiomatic expressions and new language principles, but they also learned something about writing—about expressing themselves in a natural and entertaining manner. Was three weeks too long a time for the writing of one story? Not at all. Were the children bored? Not for a minute! They loved the work and the knowledge that they were really going to produce a good story, one that they themselves would enjoy and that others would read.

The writing of stories is only one form of the use of connected language. Children should still write up news of interest to them-selves or the class, though writing a daily journal would not seem to be necessary. More letters ought to be written—to relatives, to friends who are not nearby, to sick friends and to former pupils or teachers. Children who have been to summer camps usually like to send letters to their tentmates or former camp counselors. Letters should not be written as an exercise. They should be written with the thought in mind of sending news and greetings to the recipients. Notes, such as were mentioned in the preceding chapter, should still be written. They should be perhaps a little longer and more informative.

Written accounts of trips, taken essentially for geography, science, social studies or pleasure, all give opportunity and scope for the use of language. Writing simple book reviews, or writing reasons for liking certain books or for doing certain things or for playing favorite games, all give opportunity for a telling use of language.

At Lexington School, where we have weekly assemblies, the classes occasionally write the dialogue for little skits they present. This affords opportunity for the writing of conversational language. Another popular assembly activity that utilizes vacabulary and con-nected language is the working of crossword puzzles made by some of the children. The audience is given the meaning of the needed word and then must supply it so that it can be filled in on the black-board. Many children have become quite adept at both making and solving crossword puzzles, to the betterment of their own vocabularies. Other assembly programs that the children enjoy are some that have been adapted from television (e.g. "Down You Go," "Beat the Clock") which stimulate a great interest in idioms, proverbs and colloquialisms.

Many of our assembly programs have been planned and executed by a student committee selected by the students. Each member of this committee must take over the planning and carrying out of an assembly program. In arranging for and running the program, many vital language experiences are gained. For example, the student who was arranging to show a movie at her assembly had first of all to consult with the school librarian to select an appropri-ate movie. Then she had to write letters to reserve the film, and to ask the house director to have the film picked up at the New York Public Library and returned after the showing. Notes also had to be written to the teachers informing them of the picture to be shown and requesting that they prepare their classes by familiarizing the pupils with the books on which the film was based. Finally, thank-you notes had to be sent to all who had assisted in the task of presenting the assembly program.

Pictures from newspapers, magazines or other sources still can be used as suggestions for stories. If there is an intriguing photograph in the morning paper, it can be discussed at length with the children giving their ideas as to how the people or animals feel or what they are saying. Such pictures should be used while they are fresh news if real interest is to be expected.

Another type of composition is that in which the children write out plans for an excursion, designating certain tasks to certain individuals and planning how the day is to be spent. This can be done orally or put into writing on the blackboard or posted on the bulletin board.

All children write better when they know what they are going to say before starting to write, and when they know in what order they are going to tell about things. In general this is worked out during the discussion which, as has been said, should precede all written work (except on tests). However, either a written or an oral outline should be discussed before the actual writing.

Compositions should be written on the blackboard. This provides opportunity for real teaching, for all the pupils then profit from the suggestions and corrections made on each piece of writing. No correction should ever be made without an explanation and frequently the child should be asked, "Now tell me *why* you had to add *ed*." He should then be able to answer, "Because I was writing about something that happened a long time ago." He might be asked: "Why should you need a plural pronoun?"—"Because I was talking about more than one boy." Unless a child knows *why* a correction has been made, he isn't very apt to think much about it.

The teacher who can remember the corrections she has made and explained for each child from day to day, will find that her pupils will take seriously her correction and teaching and will make an effort to remember them. Children very quickly learn which teachers are consistent in their requirements and they respond accordingly.

All through the day the teacher should be on the lookout for any and every possible occasion for putting into practice those language principles on which she has worked.

In addition to the work in composition, it is of value to have periods spent in expressing a thought in a variety of ways. This will be more valuable to the children than having them spend time on meaningless drills in the various sentence forms. There may be only slight deviations in the language, but the children gradually absorb the idea that a thought does not necessarily have to be expressed always in one way. For example, a class that had gone out with a teacher gave these versions:

This morning we went to Bloomingdale's with Miss Smith. She took us there in a taxi.

This morning Miss Smith took us to Bloomingdale's by taxi.

Our class took a trip to Bloomingdale's this morning. We went there in a taxi.

We all went to Bloomingdale's this morning. We liked going there in a taxi.

It was fun to go to Bloomingdale's in a taxi. Miss Smith treated us.

When we went to Bloomingdale's with Miss Smith we took a taxi.

Even the simplest experiences will offer opportunities for writing and rewriting sentences with the end in view of choosing the one that is expressed most interestingly. The teacher who wishes to get good compositions from her children will herself have to be interested in self-expression. Again, the teacher who feels that it takes too much time to get a worthwhile composition from her pupils will not succeed in having these pupils express themselves in a desirable manner, either in speaking or writing. Some teachers prefer the use of drills for every language period. This procedure does not make language come alive to the deaf child. It does not encourage him to improve his use of language in all his everyday affairs. So-called drills have their place in the program, but their value is in giving practice in order to fix correct forms. Drills should not be considered as an end in themselves, but as a means to better connected language.

There should be continued emphasis on the use of questions in this grade. Always, before introducing and working on new question forms, there should be a thorough review of those previously taught and constantly needed. It will take most of the year to fix the habit of correctly asking and answering such questions as: "How far is it from New York to Philadelphia?" "How long did it take John to go from his home to Boston?" "How long does it take to go to Trenton?" "How much money will it take to have a picnic?" "Which book do you want to read next?" "Which of these books belongs to Jerry?"

The only way to get the desired correct usage of these question forms is through constant, daily use. The teacher must be continually on the alert to make practical use of these questions, seeing to it that the children use them on every possible occasion and providing periods for practice and repetition of the forms needing further emphasis.

Many new verbs should be added to those the children know. I would avoid teaching any verbs in pairs or groups. For instance, I think such verbs as *to let* and *to allow* should not be taught simultaneously. *Let* is much more widely used in general conversation and is less formal than *allow*. Its correct use should be firmly established before the latter verb is added to the child's vocabulary. When it is taken up it should be carefully and explicitly explained that *allow* must be followed by the infinitive: *allow to go,* for example. Often the teacher can, by her presentation of facts, make a lasting impression on a child so that he will retain a new fact without much repetition of it. The verbs *to like, to enjoy* and *to be fond of* should not be used interchangeably nor taught at the same time, for there is a subtle difference in their meanings. We might say, "She enjoys good conversation," but I doubt if we would say, "She is fond of good conversation." Having a child use all these verbs to answer a single question can give the child the belief that any question can be answered in three ways. *This is a false idea.* To illustrate how far afield one can go in such a presentation I once observed a class of twelve-year-old boys and girls who were working on the verbs just mentioned. The teacher had sent them to the blackboard to give three answers to the question, "Do you like to make a dress?" (The question seemed a poor one! Why not ask, "Do you like to sew?") The boys and girls obligingly wrote:

Yes, I like to make a dress.
Yes, I am fond of making a dress.
Yes, I enjoy making a dress.

These children centered their thoughts on the answers they had been taught to give and not on the meaning of the language they were using. It is doubtful if any hearing person would say she was fond of making a dress—or a cake—or anything of that sort. My quarrel with the use of set drills in language principles is that too often the child doing them is merely remembering what he was told to do and gives no thought to what he is writing and gets no meaning from it. Follow-up work is necessary, but if it is to be of benefit to the child he must be aware of why he is doing it and what meaning underlies his work. I might also add that the question about making a dress was a poor one on another score. There were just as many boys in the class as there were girls. Boys of twelve do not like to make dresses! They do not enjoy sewing.

Verbs followed by a clause introduced by *that* should be stressed —think that, hope that, wish that, pretend that, make believe that. For example: "I hope that Mary can come to our party." "Do you think that Harry is sick?" "May we pretend that we are taking a trip to the zoo?"

Children have need for the past progressive tense in their conversations and writings. If this principle needs to be accented the teacher might take her class on a trip to some other part or department of the school—to the kitchen, the carpentry shop or the playground. On their return to the classroom the children could write up the experience either as a news item or in a letter. This type of introduction to the past progressive tense will have meaning for the child. If he knows the present progressive form (and he should definitely have learned that) he might mistakenly use it when telling what was going on when he was in the place about which he is writing. This would give the teacher an opening for explaining to the child and to the entire class that the activity took place before the present moment, and that since it was a continuing action at that time, and was not a completed act, the verbs should be in the past progressive—*was doing* or *were doing*. Such a trip was written up by one class as follows:

OUR TRIP TO THE CARPENTRY SHOP

Before recess we went to the carpentry shop. Everybody was busy. Mr. H. was making a table. John was painting a chair. Another boy was fixing a desk. Two boys were sitting on the floor and were waxing a coffee table. We learned a lot about the carpentry shop.

After another trip the class produced this write-up:

IN THE KITCHEN

Yesterday we all went to the kitchen. We wanted to see what was going on there. The chef was roasting a piece of meat. His helper was making a pie. A young man was washing some vegetables. A woman was paring potatoes. One of the other men was making ice cream. He gave us a taste. We liked that trip best of all!

As a follow-up, a child could be sent to some other classroom, to the library or to the office, and asked upon her return to tell the class what the people were doing in the room to which she was sent.

Miss S——— was cutting some paper.

Some children were writing and others were reading.
> or

Mrs. C———— was telling a story—or showing a film.

Talking over a visit to the zoo or a public playground, and telling what various people were doing, is always a good way to get repetition in the use of this tense.

Teachers must be careful not to confuse the teaching of the past progressive tense with the use of the verb *to see,* followed by a present participle. This is a separate language principle and should be taught as such.

When a class is using the past progressive correctly whenever indicated, and understands it and realizes that in general it follows another statement (I saw John downstairs. He was polishing his shoes.), the pupils may be introduced to the new principle—*to see* —with the present participle. This might be introduced as a way to get variety in expression. Children can say:

We watched some men. They were digging a big hole.
> or

We watched some men digging a big hole.

We saw a very little girl. She was pushing a doll carriage.
> or

We saw a very little girl pushing a doll carriage.

Later on, when the children can use relative clauses, they will have a third choice of telling of something seen. Example:

We saw a very little girl who was pushing a doll carriage.

A limited use of the present perfect tense of certain verbs should be in evidence about this time, but only incidentally. It should, of course, be brought in whenever an occasion calls for it. Children sense its meaning in such questions as:

Have you been in the hospital?
Have you written all the answers?
Have you answered every question?
Have you seen my classbook?
Where has Karen gone?
Where have you been?

Children like to play a game where one child tells of a place he has been and his partner tells whether or not he has been there.

A. I have been to Prospect Park.　B. I have never been there.
　　I've been to Central Park.　　　I've been there, too.

The same game can be played with things, places or people seen.

I have seen the Statue of Liberty.　　I've seen it too.
I've seen the Washington Monument.　I've never seen that.

On occasion the response can be, "So have I," or "I haven't."

Since more definite work will be given this year on further use of direct and indirect discourse, the past of the verbs *can, will* and *may* should be reviewed.

Children in this year should be using the simpler forms of indirect discourse—"told————that" and "said that." These forms should appear often in conversation—"My mother told me that she would bring me a present on Friday. Mary said that her mother would come to school, too." They should also appear in news and stories. At the Lexington School the children start using *told* ————*that* in the lower school. When children can use this form with a fair degree of accuracy they should not find it difficult to change from *told* to *said* when they do not mention the person addressed—when there is no *whom*.

John *told* Harry *that* he had a surprise for everyone.
John *said that* he had a surprise for every one. (no *whom*)

Under no condition should the children get practice in using indirect discourse by changing several direct quotations into indirect quotations. This is a most unnatural procedure. The repetition should come in having children tell what other people (parents, teachers, friends, counselors and others) have told them or said to them. The teacher can arrange to have people come to the classroom from time to time and tell the class about a trip they have taken, or about a place visited, or about their homes and their city or town. Later this information can be put in a letter or some other form of composition. Example:

Dear Miss Bennett,

This morning Miss Macdonald came to our class. She told us all about her trip to California and other places. She told us that she saw many tall, tall trees. She said that she saw very high mountains. Some of them were covered with snow. She told Mary that she saw her grandmother in California. She told us that the lakes were beautiful and the water was very blue.

We told Miss Macdonald that we would like to go out West. Would you?

Love from us all,
(Names)

Children can "interview" members of the staff and then make a report to the class.

Visitors can be of great help if they come from another country and are willing to tell the children something of their homeland. This information can be used at a later period by having the children repeat what the visitor told them.

Telling a chum special news items, and then telling the rest of the class what was said, can be a means of getting oral use of the principle.

"What did you tell your friend, Margie?"

"I told her that I had a good time at the party, and I told her that I would invite her to my party in April."

The teacher should, of course, use any form of indirect discourse that is called for when she is talking to the children, even though they themselves do not yet use it. For example, during the day she might have occasion to say:

I asked you to hurry up.
I told you not to waste time.
I asked Tommy where he was going.
Miss O————told me that the teachers-in-training were coming in at ten o'clock.

The children will understand the forms and they should be familiar with them in lipreading. When isolated occasions arise where a child needs one of the more difficult forms to express himself properly, it should be given to him even though it might not be taught until later.

Since indirect discourse is far from easy for the deaf child, it is best to go slowly in covering all the forms. It is far better to have one or two forms well established than to have the child exposed to all forms within the span of a few weeks. The new forms should be added when the children show need for them, but it is unlikely that they will need all of them within a very short time.

Children do not have much use for the form *told*————*to* in their oral language, for they do not go about telling people to do things. This form might more aptly appear in the writing of stories or in telling toy stories—"Mrs. Bear told her cub to stay near her." "Mrs. Bear told her baby bear to stay at home." "John told his dog to sit up and beg." "Mary told her kitten to drink the milk."

Other forms than those just mentioned will be taken up in the next chapter.

Many new phrases should be in use—*just now, in a minute, a few minutes ago, not long ago, long, long ago, often, always, a little while ago, a week ago,* and many others. Time phrases, like calendar work, should be taught through composition—oral and written.

The use of *some, any, somebody, anybody, something* and *anything* ought to be established by this time. These are not difficult. It helps very much if it is clearly explained to the children that we usually use *any, anybody, anyone* or *anything* when we are asking a question.

For example:

Have you any crayons?
Was anybody home?
Did you find anything there?
or when we are using *not*—
  I did not see anyone.
  I haven't any lollipops.
  I didn't see anything on the shelf.
It is well for any teacher of the deaf to refrain from saying, "You *never* can say that," or "You *always* must say this." The English language is so full of exceptions that no rule seems to be absolute. It is general for people to use *some, someone, somebody* or *something* when they are making a positive statement.
  Someone is at the door.
  There is something for you in your locker.
  There are some new books on the shelf.
I should be inclined to follow this rule for it helps the children to have some sort of guide.

There is one other language principle I should like to take up at this point. It is the use of prepositional phrases modifying the subject or the object of a sentence. Before taking this up with the class for detailed study, the teacher should make sure that the children are familiar with the meaning of the question form *which*. This is the principle we use most often in telling which of two or more things we prefer. (I like the coat *with pockets* better than the coat *without pockets*.)

Before going into direct teaching the teacher should use the form in her conversation and in stories. Example:

Mary's grandmother gave her two dolls for her birthday. One doll had curly hair and the other doll had short, straight hair. Mary likes the doll *with curly hair* the most.

Later a similar story could be told and the class allowed to tell which of the things in question they think Mary liked better.

Mary's aunt gave her two sweaters for Christmas. One sweater had no collar and one had a cute little collar. Which sweater do you think was Mary's favorite?

Some may think she preferred the sweater without a collar while others may think she liked the one with the collar. In either case the children use a prepositional phase.

The children can make up stories, too, and incorporate the language into their stories and other written work. They will also receive practice by answering such questions as: "Which book have you? The book with pictures or the book without pictures?" "Which plant did you water? The one on my desk or the one on the window sill?"

NATURAL LANGUAGE FOR DEAF CHILDREN

Since it is easier to use a phrase modifying the object, it would seem best to concentrate on that use until the children have no difficulty with it. When they know this use, the use of a phrase modifying the subject could be introduced. (The hat on the desk belongs to Harold. The doll in the box is Helen's. The book with the red cover is missing.)

A limited use of the *when* clause should be evident in the oral and written work of the class—that is the use of *when* with a past tense verb in both the independent and dependent clause. (I *saw* the circus when I *was* small. I *played* in the fields when I *was* in the country.) Any child likes to talk about what he did when he was a baby. (I *drank* milk from a bottle when I *was* a baby. I *rode* in a carriage when I *was* very small.) He might tell about when he was at the beach (I *dug* a hole in the sand when I *was* at Coney Island.), or when he was at camp, or visiting a relative. There are endless things for a child to talk about, and in doing so to use a clause introduced by *when*. The teacher should word her questions and remarks in such a way as to keep the *when* in the right place. If a child writes, "When I saw the Hunter College girls I looked out of the window," he should be asked, "What did you do first?" He replies, "I looked out of the window." Then he should be taught that the *when* must go with what happened first and he can correct himself. "I saw the Hunter College girls when I looked out of the window."

The other rules for *when* clauses might be needed on occasion, and demanded, and I would give the child the right form but would not go into detailed work on all rules for *when* clauses at this time. The children will have the greatest use for the first rule (past verb— when—past verb), and they will need a great deal of practice in using it. A warning—do not give the rule and have children write sentences to illustrate it! This is not a natural way of using the principle. When we teach deaf children anything in language we do so because we hope they will have this language whenever and wherever they need to use it. All their work on language should lead to this fulfillment.

There are innumerable language principles that must be taught during any school year, many more than those I have mentioned. I have tried to touch upon those that most teachers find troublesome. If all teaching is approached in a normal and natural manner, and if emphasis is put on understanding and use of what has been taught, the teacher cannot go very far wrong.

CHAPTER VIII

GROWING IN INDEPENDENCE

Most wonderful of all are words, and how
they make friends one with another. . .

WILLIAM SYDNEY PORTER
Strictly Business

A QUOTATION from Dora V. Smith bears great weight when talking
about the teaching of language to the deaf:

> The further the child progresses in the elementary school the
> greater is the danger that his language period may degenerate
> into one of exercise-doing, learning words in columns out of
> context, or studying language forms, divorced from the use he
> is making of language during the rest of the day. Special care,
> therefore, needs to be exercised to continue the kind of rich pro-
> gram of well-motivated enterprises common in the lower grades
> in order that the growth of language may continue in relation-
> ship to the development of meaning and that the challenge of a
> social purpose may motivate expression. Then the needed reme-
> dial drill and positive instruction in word knowledge and
> linguistic forms may be related directly to the problems which
> confront the pupil in his daily use of language.[1]

The teacher of the deaf would do well to ponder these words! If
the hearing child, with his widespread understanding and use of
language, needs to have exercises and drills that are directly connected with the daily use of language, how much more so does the
deaf child need to concentrate on ideas rather than on cut and dried
drill. He *does* need work to supply repetition of correct usage of
all the language forms that he will be required to use, but first of
all he must be aware of the reason and need for such work as a
follow-up of the language he has had need of in order to express

---

[1]Smith, Dora V., "Growth in Language Power as Related to Child Develop-
ment," in *Teaching Language in the Elementary School* (43rd Yearbook, Part
II, National Society for the Study of Education). Chicago: University of Chicago
Press, 1944, p. 59.

himself clearly and correctly. He needs to be able to write about what is going on in his mind. He needs language to tell of things he knows, and things he thinks about—his interests, his fears, his problems. For these reasons he should be taught the kind of language by which he can live—live happily, wholesomely and satisfactorily.

Children of twelve and thirteen years of age have far-reaching interests. Not only have their school studies advanced to cover a much broader range of information and a greater knowledge of the world about them, but their own personal activities have branched out in many directions. They belong to clubs and to Scout troops; they go to parties and have picnics; they take educational trips; they often travel to and from school alone or in the school bus; they make things for themselves and presents for other people; they take part in assembly programs; give plays or skits in the playrooms; they enter into the sports program with great enthusiasm; they become collectors of stamps, postcards and other things of interest to boys and girls of their own age. In short, they develop the same interests and desires and take part in the same activities as do their hearing contemporaries. They are just as independent and just as full of initiative as are their peers.

With this ever-expanding need for a growing vocabulary, the teacher must find every possible way in which to give to the child the ability to use correctly the language he needs to cover all his experiences and to do so in a natural and interesting manner. She must give him confidence in his use of language, and also pleasure in it. To do this she will have to be alert to, and sympathetic with, the day-by-day language needs of each and every child in her class. She must take a friendly interest in the life of each child and learn to detect the individual needs and interests as well as those of the group. No two children are exactly alike, either in their needs or their abilities. While many of the class activities allow for group teaching and participation, there will still be need for individual work. The gifted child will need an enriched program; the not-so-gifted child will need to be helped with extra periods of structured follow-up work on the language principles in which he is weak.

On many occasions it will be necessary for the teacher to set up an environment where she can teach the language needed for certain occasions—greetings and response to greetings, for example, or expressions of interest in what others are saying. The deaf child must be *taught* the social graces that are practiced by hearing children his own age—how to act and what to say at a tea, or in a public eating place, or as a guest in a home; how to act and what to say when visiting a sick person, particularly an adult; what to say when given a prize or a gift; what to say to the storekeeper, the bus driver, the saleswoman, the paper boy, the librarian, or any of the people with whom the child has dealings. The deaf are frequently accused of being tactless, rude and unfeeling when the problem is actually one of lack of language. The fault lies not with them but with those who neglected to teach them the proper responses or remarks necessary in meeting situations that call for tact, sympathy and thoughtfulness. The right language at the right time, for each and every situation, cannot be picked up by the young deaf child. Some of it must be taught to him and in a way that will be used by him naturally, spontaneously and graciously. It should be the aim of every teacher to help each child to grow up to be a loved and respected member of society, not just an acceptable member of it.

Children who are entering the teen-age period are usually very conscious of themselves and of the things they do and how they do them. They want to be accepted in every way. This is an inducement to them to strive for a better and more correct use of language. When they do accomplish this they find great satisfaction in speaking and writing English. However, acquiring an effective use of English is not an easy task for either the deaf or the hearing child. It requires hard work on the part of the teacher as well as on the part of the child.

The teacher of the deaf must not be limited to a mere concern with the use of language as a means of self-expression. She should also be concerned with the use and knowledge of the various language forms and principles, so difficult for the deaf child to master. The teacher of hearing children must constantly *correct* the language used by her pupils, while the teacher of the deaf must *develop* the language of her pupils from the ground up. There is a vast difference in the techniques necessary in handling these two problems. The deaf child has much to learn that the hearing child knows by the simple process of hearing over and over again words and sentences, and understanding their meanings. When one considers the task of teaching language to the deaf, it is not easy to keep from being overwhelmed. Yet the deaf child of average ability can learn the English language. How far beyond the ordinary uses he can go depends upon himself as well as his teacher. The gifted deaf child will go very far if he has a teacher who can nurture his gifts. Each child must accomplish the most of which he is capable.

In the group we shall now be thinking about, the conversation time at the opening of the school day should be varied according to the immediate interests of the children. At this time many idiomatic responses can be taught and colloquial expressions learned. The latter should be part of the deaf child's oral vocabulary if he is not to be singled out for his stiff and unnatural manner of speaking. It bears repeating that the length of time devoted to the early conversation period should vary according to the enthusiasms and activities of the children at the moment. This should be the time for learning how to converse—for sharing news, for disclosing information and for revealing personal problems when they exist. This is a good way to start the day. Naturally there will be talk about various matters all through the day, for there should be discussions about subjects being studied, compositions of all kinds that are to be written, greetings to visitors, if any, and innumerable occasions when the children should speak up and be heard.

If deaf children are to write naturally and correctly they should *think* in natural and correct English. The language they use should be real to them. It must be alive.

Deaf pupils who have spent seven years in the regular school program should have a clear understanding and use of a vocabulary sufficient to describe their ordinary experiences and activities, express their usual needs or ask ordinary questions. This they should do in correct English. If this is so, the teacher should be able to start the study of more advanced composition and consider these specific points—choice of words, clearer expression, correct expression in larger units, and more complex sentence forms.

It is important, before taking up the longer composition, that the teacher discover what things are most vital to the pupils in her class. She will never get good compositions unless she makes this study first. Subjects for composition must be personal, definite and sufficiently brief to allow for discussion on the quality of the writing, which is necessary if the pupils are to go very far in the way of achievement.

As pupils learn to criticize the compositions of others, it is well to stress the fact that criticism means the noting of particularly good points as well as of poor work or errors. The children should be objective about suggestions for better words, different language constructions, more interesting or more arresting opening sentences. Good class criticism helps all the pupils and can be made an inspiration for better compositions.

Letters and notes should be written whenever occasions call for them. They should be longer, more interesting and better written than in previous years and should include, in addition to those already mentioned, notes of sympathy, congratulation and appreciation.

Book reviews, notices of events to take place, write-ups of assembly programs and other forms of entertainment, reports on activities, and giving information and directions through articles for the bulletin board, should all be part of the language program.

Writing short stories suggested by pictures, newspaper items or happenings within the experiences of the children can be made the basis for the teaching of new vocabulary and new language principles and for developing better ways of expressing one's self. There must be constant striving on the part of the pupils to express themselves more and more interestingly and intelligently. They must become aware of good composition and recognize it when they see it.

Such personal experiences as getting lost, being frightened, receiving a surprise, having accidents, or funny experiences also furnish material for compositions, as do descriptions of people met, accidents seen and interesting things observed on the street.

It is amazing to see how great an interest deaf children will take in learning to express themselves well, and what contributions they will make to a general discussion of, let us say, beginning or topic sentences. Not so long ago I was teaching a class of thirteen-year-olds who were starting out on a project that would become a collection of stories about a young teen-age girl. The children had previously decided on a name for the girl and on her age. We decided we would write about a birthday surprise, each pupil deciding what the surprise was to be in her particular story.

We used the title, "The Birthday." Then we talked about the opening sentence. We considered whether Mary Anne, for that was the name given to the "heroine," would get up early on her birthday or stay in bed and sleep late. It was conceded by one and all that Mary Anne probably would rise early on her fourteenth birthday, so we talked about expressions that meant rising early. Some of these were: *up with the birds, at the crack of dawn, up with the sun.* Then we talked about Mary Anne's getting up—whether or not she would need an alarm or would have to be awakened.

Our topic sentences were finally written on the third day. Here are some of them.

Mary Anne was up with the birds on October third.

No one had to waken Mary Anne on Saturday, October third.

Mary Anne got up at the crack of dawn on October 3rd.

It didn't take an alarm clock to waken Mary Anne on the third of October.

The first one up at 35 Main Street on October 3rd was Mary Anne.

Mary Anne got up very early on October the third.

Mary Anne was up when the cock crowed one morning.

All these contributions were discussed; some were altered and new ones were added.

The next step was to develop the topic sentence. This took several days, working for forty-five or fifty minutes each day. The second sentence was to tell why Mary Anne had risen so early. Examples:

It was her fourteenth birthday and she was excited about it.

She was all agog with excitement because it was her birthday and she had many plans.

She could hardly wait to go downstairs to see her birthday presents.

It was her birthday and she expected a new bicycle from her daddy.

She wanted to see her birthday gifts because she was fourteen years old that day.

It was her birthday and she had a lot of work to do.

The compositions gradually developed, and then it was time to work on a good ending. The children talked about how they felt after a very happy and exciting day, what they did when all the excitement was over, and how they felt "inside." Some of the closing sentences were:

Mary Anne waved good-bye to her friends. Then she hugged her mother and said, "Oh, what a lovely birthday! Thank you very much."

"Such a happy birthday, Mommy. I loved everything," said Mary Anne.

"This is the best birthday I've ever had," Mary Anne said at bedtime.

When Mary Anne's friends had left she said, "What a wonderful birthday I've had!"

Mary Anne was full of happiness at the end of her fourteenth birthday.

One of the stories, not the best, but average for the class follows:

THE BIRTHDAY

Mary Anne Smith was up with the birds on October third. It was her birthday and she had a lot of work to do because she was going to have a big party that evening. She was fourteen years old now and she was very happy.

The family was not awake when Mary Anne went downstairs but she did not mind. She fixed some breakfast for herself. Then she peeked into the living room. There were no presents there. Mary Anne wondered about her presents, but she was not worried.

Mary Anne thought she would help her mother. She ran the vacuum over the rug in the living room. That woke up the whole family. They did not care. When they came downstairs they wished Mary Anne a happy birthday and gave her their presents. "Such wonderful presents!" said Mary Anne. "I love all of them." Her father said "You haven't seen mine. It's out on the porch." Mary Anne dashed to the porch. She cried, "Oh, brother!" when she saw a beautiful bicycle. She gave her father a bear's hug.

Mary Anne helped her mother all morning. She washed and dried dishes, she dusted the living room and the dining room and she ironed napkins for the party.

That evening seven boys and seven girls came to the party. They had a delightful time. They played games and had wonderful refreshments. Most of them had presents for Mary Anne and she liked them very much. When her friends had left Mary Anne said, "What a wonderful birthday I've had! Thank you, everybody."

Not all stories need be long. The compositions children write for a "book" are usually longer than other compositions.

From time to time the pupils wrote other stories about Mary Anne. She took trips, she paid a visit to her grandmother's farm, she visited New York City. She was ill and had to stay in bed for a week, she won a prize at school, she went to a Girl Scout party. In fact, Mary Anne entered into many activities that interest fourteen-year-old girls. Was the time spent on these compositions worthwhile from the standpoint of language skills? It was, definitely! The children learned many new words, idioms and casual expressions. They learned better, more interesting and more varied ways of expressing a thought. Since each story was discussed first of all by the entire class, all the children profited by the contributions of individual pupils, all learned something about good writing and worthwhile oral discussion. If the teacher and her class are sincerely interested in the work they are doing, no time can be lost. If language constructions needing attention crop up, the teacher can explain these usages of language at the time and at a later period take them up in more detail. It has always seemed to me to be better procedure to take several days on one piece of composition than to have children write many inconsequential pieces of connected language, since these are usually done with little or no real preparation and provide no learning situations. Deaf children need inspiration for writing rather than cold facts of no general interest to themselves or anybody else.

Collections of stories, such as the one just mentioned, are of interest long after their completion. Children like to read them over and over, have other children read them, and eventually take them home. In this way many of the common expressions and idioms become part of the child's spoken and written fund of language. Another value of this type of teaching English is that the pupils enjoy what other members of the class have written and often make suggestions to one another as to changes in the compositions. When the use of language becomes part of a child's daily living, when he uses it as a matter of course and because he wants to, then we may say that the child "has language." If he uses words only in exercises or only in stereotyped form, then he does not "have language."

The teacher who wants her children to have a useful and satisfying command of English will find many ways of providing the tools so necessary to the deaf if they are to express themselves easily, correctly, interestingly and happily. She must *believe* that this skill can be acquired by the deaf. She must continually study to improve her own techniques, both in writing and in teaching. It is inevitable that children will reflect their teachers. Therefore the teacher must set the pace and become a model worth emulating. A teacher who does not care, or know very much about teaching language will never succeed in developing a good use of language by her pupils. If the teacher is not enthusiastic, neither will her pupils be enthusiastic. In any subject, the teacher will not be very successful unless she enjoys what she is teaching. Children know without being told what a teacher's enthusiasms are. This is true whether the children are five or fifteen. Through the teaching of language deaf children learn much about themselves, other people, their own environment, their own capabilities, the world without and the world within. Because this is true, the deaf child of any age needs a teacher who can, through her teaching, make the life of the deaf child not a bane but a blessing.

I would like to suggest here that for the teacher starting out in the teaching of composition, it is sometimes helpful to use a language arts textbook series such as those listed in Chapter XI of this book. Some of these books give suggestions for developing good writing, and they give examples of composition work of various types.

What about the work in language principles for the twelve- and thirteen-year-olds? There will be many new language constructions and forms needing to be worked out and learned by the children. All errors in language usage that appear in compositions should be noted and taken up in a special period. Careful explanation of the language principle should be made and constructive exercises worked out so that the pupils can get the repetition required if they are to fix the habit of correct usage.

If there is a rule that will help a child, I should give it to him to help him in the beginning and until he has mastered the language principle that has troubled him. For example, the rule for *when* clauses might help a child to get his verb tenses straight. Unfortunately, there are many English constructions for which there are no definite and clear rules. There are instances where there is nothing to do but give a child the correct form and insist that he remember it. If he is to remember it, the teacher must be sure he has some need for it and some personal interest in it. She must provide work that will give him the opportunity to use that particular language over and over again.

Harry Allan Overstreet says in *About Ourselves:* "Children must, indeed, take in information. But, in the first place they must want to take it in or somehow be induced really to want it. In the second place, it must be such information as lures them on."[2] Our word for this is motivation. It seems to me that much that has been said about learning by doing, as it applies to carrying on all work in language, presupposes the perfect teacher and the almost perfect child. Nevertheless, the teacher of the deaf is, because of the nature of her task, eminently fitted to teach language by means of *doing* things which demand verbal expression. It is also true that the average deaf child *does* want to know how to express himself in correct language and is happy when he can do so.

The pupils in the middle grades should be using longer sentences in both their speaking and writing. Perfecting the simple sentence by the use of adjectives, prepositional phrases or adverbs is but one way of making the child's language clearer and more interesting. Using complex sentences is another way. The use of clauses introduced by *when* is one of the language principles needing special attention. We spoke of the simplest use of a *when* clause in our last chapter; that is, the use of a past verb in both the independent

[2]Overstreet, H. A., *About Ourselves; Psychology for Normal People.* New York: W. W. Norton & Company, Inc., c1927, p. 170.

and dependent clauses. If the children understand the meaning of the habitual tense of verbs, they should be ready for the use of the *when* clause having a verb in the present tense in each clause. (I *help* mother when I *am* at home. Granny always *brings* me a present when she *comes* to our house.) The two forms just mentioned are not difficult for the child. It is the third rule for the use of the *when* clause that is difficult for him. He assumes that if the verbs in the clauses agree when used in the past tense, and again when used in the present tense, they will also agree if the future tense is being used. He therefore wants to say, "I *shall work* with Daddy when I *shall be* home next week." It should be impressed upon him that the third rule is unlike the first two and he must remember this. To give facility in using the form the children might tell what they will do when they are at home, at camp, visiting someone or shopping at some store. (I *will* learn to swim when I *am* at camp. Mary *will play* on the beach when she *stays* with her aunt. Mother *will buy* me new shoes when we *shop* at Macy's on Saturday.)

The use of *if* as a connective is very difficult and I should not take it up at this level. The children should have a clear concept of the conditional nature of the word through the teacher's use of it.

You may go if you've finished your work.
We'll go to the museum if Miss V——— says that we may.
We will take the sled if it isn't too heavy.
You may use the glue if you are very careful with it.

All forms of indirect discourse should be mastered during the year. They should not be taught too closely together, for children need much practice in using one form before taking up a new one.

The teacher should be cognizant of the underlying rules for use of indirect discourse. Crowell's *Dictionary of English Grammar and Handbook of American Usage* makes the following statement on the sequence of tenses—the relationship of tenses in subordinate clauses as related to principal clauses:

> There must be logical and grammatical agreement of tenses, as "He *says* that it *is* too late; yesterday he *said* that it *was* too early."
>
> In statements of principle or universal fact the present is commonly used, as "You have heard that honesty *is* the best policy."
>
> If the principal verb is present or future, the subordinate verbs may be in any tense, as "I *understand* that he *has come* but *will* soon *go* again."
>
> Verbs are said to be in *natural sequence* when they show the logical time relation, as "I wonder if he will come," and in *attracted sequence* when the subordinate verb must change form to

agree with the principal verb, as "I *am* tired," he said, becomes "He said that he *was* tired."[3]

Before branching out into the use of the verb, *to ask,* the teacher should make sure that the children understand that when they use *told that* the verb in the following clause is also a "past" verb. If they know this rule and practice it, they should not have difficulty in applying the *past* tense of verbs when they use the form *asked if.*

One way to get repetition in the use of this particular form is to have pupils ask some individual guest or other person questions on a definite subject, such as a trip. At a later time they can tell or write what they asked the person. For example:

This morning Miss B———— told us all about her trip to California. We asked her many questions.
John asked her if she went in a car. She said, "Yes."
Helen asked her if she went alone. She told her that she went with her mother.
Mary asked her if she had a fine time. She said that she did.
Harold asked her if she saw any bears. She told him that she had seen many.
Bobby asked her if she met any Indians. She said, "No."

Another way to provide practice in the use of the form is to have the children tell in class what they asked other children when they were in the playroom, yard or dormitory. Example:

MARY: "I asked Harold if he saw the movie about the wild animals."
JOHN: "I asked Helen if she had an eraser."
HARRY: "I asked Bobby if he liked the new boy."
JULIA: "I asked Ruth if she wanted to play with me."

Children enjoy writing about questions asked by someone outside the classroom. For example:

Miss M———— asked me if I liked the picture.
Mr. J———— asked me if I wanted to play basketball.

Practice can also be provided by reading a story and later telling or writing what one person in the book said, told, or asked someone else:

The mother asked her little girl if she wanted to go downtown. The little girl told her that she wanted to play at home.

There are many ways of getting practice in using indirect discourse without resorting to the unnatural procedure of changing direct quotations to indirect quotations. For example, the teacher might tell a very simple story, using direct quotations, and then check on the story.

---

[3]Weseen, Maurice H., *Crowell's Dictionary of English Grammar and Handbook of American Usage.* New York: Thomas Y. Crowell Company, c1928, p. 573.

TEACHER: "What did Mrs. Smith tell her little boy?"
CHILD: "She told him that the family would go on a picnic."
TEACHER: "That's right. Now tell me what the little boy asked his mother."
CHILD: "He asked her if she wanted him to help her."

The form *asked if* should be fixed in the minds of the children before other forms are introduced and worked on, *but* if a child wants to ask a question that does not begin with "Did —?", he should be given the correct form:

I asked the new boy where he lived. I asked Mr. S. when we were going to the ball game.

The verb *asked,* followed by where, when, how, what color, why —is not difficult for the average deaf child once it has been made clear to him that he must use the simple past of the verb after these connectives.

We *asked* Mary *where* she *found* the pen.
We *asked* her *when* she *got* the book.
We *asked* her *how* she *liked* the story.
We *asked* Harold *why* he *stayed* at home.
We *asked* him *how* he *made* the box.

If a child has trouble with these forms it sometimes helps to write in a column what the person addressed did.

What John did:
1. He went to the country.
   We *asked* John *when* he went to the country.
2. He stayed on a farm.
   We *asked* him *why* he stayed on a farm.
3. He saw a bull.
   We *asked* him *where* he saw a bull.
4. He watered the horses.
   We *asked* him *how* he watered the horses.

A more advanced approach to the interviewing of adults and reporting on these interviews will also provide use of indirect discourse.

Let me sound a note of caution regarding the teaching of indirect discourse: Don't go too fast. Children will often become confused if new forms are added before they can use correctly the previously taught forms.

Special work will be needed at this time on the use of the present perfect tense of some of the verbs the children require in their expanding use of language. The children must not only learn this tense but they must learn *when* its use is called for. The simplest use of the present perfect tense is that wherein an action is completed but no time stressed.

I have finished my work.
I have seen that.
John has been to the hospital.
The man has washed all the windows.

The children should absorb the fact that *when* doesn't matter in the above sentences. When the time *is* given the simple past should be used.

I finished my work last night.
I saw that yesterday.
John went to the hospital last Sunday.
The man washed all the windows on Saturday.

A second use of this tense would be with such time phrases as *ever, never, often, seldom* and *always*.

We have never gone to Jones Beach.
Mary has never been to the circus.
I have often visited Johnny.
I have always thought that—
Have you ever been there?

A good way to start pupils using this form is to have them talk about things they have often done or seen, or never done or seen. Also the tense can be used in stories told and in silent reading. It should crop up continually in conversation.

The third and most difficult use of the present perfect tense is that in which it is used for an action completed before the present time, but extending from some time in the past up to the present.

I have been in this school for ten years.
Miss M. has been my sewing teacher for three years.

Once the pupils have learned the meaning and use of this tense they should be encouraged and reminded to use it in their conversation and in their compositions whenever it applies.

I have broken my glasses.
John has spilled the ink.
The fire bell has just rung.
Harry has gone to the hospital.
May I go? I have never been there.

The children will receive much help from talking about pictures. A picture of a baby crying might inspire this question and answer: "Why do you think the baby is crying?" "She has dropped her bottle or her mother has left her alone."

Each year pupils in the middle grades should acquire a more comprehensive use of the infinitive used as the object of a verb— *to like to read, to try to write nicely, to pretend to study, to want to eat, would like to rest, wishes to speak,* and many others as they develop day by day.

115

Only constant repetition will fix the habit of correctly using such verbs as *put on, take off, pick up.* The difficulty in handling these verbs comes when a pronoun is the object and the child does not know that the pronoun must precede the preposition. This should be explained to him, and multiple uses cited:

I saw a dime on the sidewalk. I picked it up and put it in my pocket.
Mary's mother bought Mary a beautiful coat. Mary put it on to show her friend.
Harry dropped his glove. Johnny picked it up.
Harry tried on his new shoes. Then he took them off and put them away.

If a child can correctly use one of these "double verbs," he should have no trouble with new ones that come up as his use of language increases.

Much more definite work should be done on the use of adjectives. The pupils should know the three degrees of comparison (positive, comparative and superlative) of those adjectives they use in oral or written work, and they should understand the reasons for their use. It is well to start the comparison of adjectives by listing many of the regular ones first, for these are less difficult—big, bigger, biggest; strong, stronger, strongest; tall, taller, tallest. When the children have a clear understanding of just what comparison means, and of when each form is called for, they should take up the comparison of irregular adjectives. I should not have them compare adjectives that were not going to be used at this time, but would confine the work to those that the children would find useful. There are certain rules for spelling which the children must master. For example:

1. In adjectives that end in silent *e,* the *e* must be dropped before *er* or *est* is added—fine, finer, finest.
2. Where adjectives end in *y,* the *y* must be changed to *i* before the endings *er* and *est*—happy, happier, happiest.
3. Adjectives that contain a short vowel and end in a single consonant must have the consonant doubled before the endings *er* and *est*—fat, fatter, fattest.

The foregoing rules should be learned through their application and not merely be memorized.

The most difficult adjectives to compare are those where more and most must be prefixed to the positive degree.

beautiful, more beautiful, most beautiful
splendid, more splendid, most splendid

Children must remember that most adjectives of two or more syllables are compared in the above manner.

Then, of course, there are those adjectives that are compared by the use of different words:

good	better	best

Pupils should always transfer into connected language all adjectives they are asked to compare. They should be shown that in comparing two things as to size one may be larger than the other and yet neither would be really large in the ordinary sense of the word. They should not compare two things that have no quality in common, such as sugar and vinegar.

Concepts of comparison are very difficult for the deaf child to acquire, and it is good policy to go slowly in all work in comparison of adjectives. Being able to compare long lists of adjectives from memory is no indication that the deaf child has a real understanding of these forms and will use them correctly when the need for them presents itself.

Such phrases of comparison as *as sweet as sugar, as dark as night, as good as gold,* should be taught through conversation and reading.

Adverbs the children use in their daily work should be compared so that all three forms will be available to them. For example:

fast	faster	fastest
early	earlier	earliest
carefully	more carefully	most carefully

There will be many new language principles needing attention as the children attempt to speak and write in ever-widening units of connected language. I have not attempted to cite all the language principles the teacher should introduce and teach at this time. She should be guided by the language needs of her particular group of children as indicated in their spoken and written attempts to express themselves. No two classes are ever alike in their needs. It is the teacher's responsibility to meet the needs of her particular class rather than to conform to an established order and presentation of the teaching of language principles at a certain time in a certain grade. If all is going well with her class, the pupils will be showing her the things they need and want to know, and they will do this through their interests, curiosity, and growing awareness of how very important language is in every phase of their lives.

Teachers must take from the writings of their pupils certain language principles that need clarification and intensive repetitive work in order to fix the habit of correct usage.

One troublesome language principle is the use of the passive voice. Unless carefully taught, deaf pupils will use it where it is not called for. Children who are given exercises in which sentences in the active voice must be changed into the passive voice are bound to be confused. They believe that the two forms are interchangeable and that either can be used. This is not so! When children write, "My purse was lost by me," or, "The doll was held by me," it should be evident that they do not understand when the passive voice is called for. Many years ago I saw a demonstration of the teaching of the passive voice which illustrates how far wrong a teacher can be in presenting this particular language principle. A boy was asked to pass a box of candies. When this had been done, his teacher said, "Tell me what you did." The lad replied, "I passed the candy," which was a natural expression for his action. Then the teacher said, "Now tell me about the candy." I hoped he would say, "It was good." However, he dutifully answered as he had been taught, "The candy was passed by me." To my mind, the children in that class were not really learning about the uses of the passive voice but merely the form.

What pupils *should learn* is that we use the passive voice for the following reasons:

1. To describe a state of being or condition.
    My shoes are worn out.
    Harry was embarrassed.
2. (a) In speaking of things usually done where the agent is unknown or immaterial.
         Our clothes are washed in the school laundry.
         The classrooms are swept every day.
    (b) In speaking of exceptional happenings.
         The room has not been swept.
         Little wheat was raised last year.
3. (a) To report important events such as accidents and widespread destruction.
         The car skidded into a tree and the driver was injured.
         Hundreds of people were killed in the earthquake.
         A great deal of property was destroyed by the floods in Pennsylvania.
    (b) To report events of importance to individuals.
         I was not invited to the reception.
         The man was arrested and taken to jail.

Pupils who know the "why and wherefore" of the language forms they use are far less apt to misuse them than are those children who merely try to remember forms and incorporate them into their written work without understanding them. Let us take, for example, the use of the past perfect tense. Too many deaf children misuse this tense because they think it means just a past time. This we know is a wrong concept. The past perfect tense is used when we wish to show which of two events or actions happened first, when the natural order is reversed. Some grammars define it thus: "The past perfect tense denotes that the action was completed at some point in past time." The teacher should impress upon her pupils the fact that the past and the past perfect tenses are not synonomous.

In simple narration there is little use for this tense, since events discussed are usually told in the order of their occurrence. Yet even in the lower grades children have occasions to use the past perfect tense, and when such is the case, the child should be given the form with a simple explanation. A young child might write: "One of our turtles was on the table when we came to school this morning. It crawled out of its box. It was dead." He should then and there be given the form *had crawled* with the explanation that the turtle *had crawled* out before the children *came* in. If a child has visualized a condition, it will not confuse him when he is given the correct form to express that condition; on the contrary, the association of the verb form with a live situation which stimulated a need for the expression will make a vivid impression, though the child may be unconscious of the fact at the time.

A great many of the errors made by the deaf in the use of verbs are due to faulty presentation and to unrealistic exercises which do not give the child the right concepts of these verbs. The writing of many sentences that incorporate a language principle will not be of much value if the child's attention is centered only on the principle to be used. If he has been given many experiences in the telling of which he must make use of newly taught language principles, this new knowledge will be used understandingly.

Before pupils reach the last few years of school they should have acquired a clear understanding and a correct use of those language principles that are necessary to express themselves in good English. If they have not done so, the work in language in the upper grades will be mediocre, to say the least, and the pupils will not be prepared to move into the advanced work of these grades.

I am closing this chapter with a complete lesson in composition, conducted by Mrs. Margaret Wood with a class of children varying in age from 11-and-a-half to 12-and-a-half years. These children entered school at three years of age. Three have I.Q.'s under 100, three are just over 100, and others are 112, 114 and 118. Two of the children have good usable hearing when wearing an aid, and the others are typically deaf children. All are good lipreaders.

The lesson was taken down verbatim, in shorthand. No changes have been made. The compositions were written on the blackboard and corrections and criticism were made with all pupils participating.

(Two pictures were used. One showed a little girl preparing to strike a ball, with laughing boys in the background. The second picture showed the girl after she had batted the ball, and in the background the boys are staring with mouths agape.)

TEACHER'S AIM

To guide the children in writing an interesting story from a picture series.

MOTIVATION

TEACHER: Do you like baseball?
CHILDREN: Yes.
TEACHER: Can you play baseball?
CHILDREN: Yes.
TEACHER: I have a cute set of pictures of some children playing baseball and we are going to write a story from them. (*Showed the first picture to the group*) Isn't it funny?
CHILDREN: Yes.

LESSON

TEACHER: What do you think the girl said to the boys? You may give her any name you wish.
FRANCES: Jan asked the boys if they would let her to play baseball with them.
TEACHER: There's a mistake in your sentence.
MARCIA: Take out *to*.
TEACHER: That's right.
MARCIA: Jan asked the boys if she could play baseball with them.
REBA: Debbie thought that she could play baseball very well.
TEACHER: Good. But what do you think she said?
SHARON: She asked the boys if she could play with them.
TEACHER: Put both sentences together.
SHARON: Debbie thought that she could play baseball very well so she asked the boys if she could play with them.
TEACHER: That's a better sentence.
JAN: Shirley thought and tried to ask the boys to play with them.
TEACHER: Is that a good sentence?
CHILDREN: No.
TEACHER: What do you think happened?
BARBARA: Cynthia was walking by the playground. She saw a group of boys playing baseball. She watched them and then she went over to ask them if she could play with them. She bragged that she could play well. They didn't believe her. They laughed and . . .
TEACHER: Do you know the word *snickered?*
BARBARA: They laughed and snickered at her

TEACHER: Very good. Be thinking of what the catcher said to the pitcher.

BEVERLY: One day after school Jane was going home and she saw the boys was playing baseball.

TEACHER: You have a mistake.

BARBARA: Omit *was* before *playing.*

TEACHER: (*Explained to Beverly why she didn't need* was *playing.*)

BEVERLY: One day after school Jane was going home and she saw the boys playing baseball on the school field. She decided that she wanted to watch the boys' game. Then she thought that she wanted to play. She walked over to the captain and asked him if she could play. He said, "No girls are allowed." She pleaded with him and he gave her a chance. When it was time for her to hit, the boys made fun of her.

TEACHER: That's good work.

SHARON: One day Janey saw the boys playing baseball. She wanted to play with them. She went over to the boys and asked if she could play. They told her that she could not because she was no good and she was too young. She begged the boys to let her play. They were disgusted with her, but they said she could have one chance.

TEACHER: I like that.

SECOND DAY

JAN: One day Susie Q was playing with her friends on the playground. When she was playing with them, she saw some boys playing baseball. She was supposed to go home, but she wanted to play with the boys.

BEVERLY: She wanted to play with the boys *instead.*

TEACHER: That's a good idea.

JAN: She met the captain and asked if she could play with them.

TEACHER: That's the same as Beverly's idea. See if you can get a different one.

JAN: The boys asked her to prove to them that she could play.

TEACHER: See if you can make your work different from the others.

MARCIA: One morning . . .

TEACHER: Don't begin your paragraphs in the same way—one day —one time—one morning.

MARCIA: One morning Susan went to the playground to meet her friends. She played with them all morning. Then she noticed the boys playing on the baseball field.

TEACHER: Why don't you take out *one morning?*

REBA: On Saturday Debbie went for a walk. She walked by the baseball field and she saw the boys playing baseball. She watched them. She said that she could play very well.

BARBARA M: She went over to ask the boys if she could play with them. They did not believe that she could play but they told her she could have one hit.

PAT: One turn at bat.

TEACHER: That's a good idea. We have talked about the first picture enough. Most of you have the idea and know the language that you need to write about it so we will talk about the next picture. Look at it and see what has happened. Can the girl play ball?

CHILDREN: Yes.

TEACHER: Look at the boys. How do they feel?

CHILDREN: Surprised.

TEACHER: Tell what you think happened.

BARBARA M.: When the pitcher threw the ball, Angela hit the ball.

TEACHER: I don't like *the ball* again.

REBA: It.

TEACHER: That's right.

BARBARA M.: When the pitcher threw the ball, Angela hit it. The boys were so surprised.

TEACHER: The language is correct, but do you think it is very exciting? Look at the picture. The girl is thrilled and the boys can't believe their eyes. Try to get more feeling of surprise and excitement in the paragraph.

REBA: When the pitcher threw the ball, Debbie hit it very hard and it went over the fence.

TEACHER: That's better. I like the last part of your sentence very much.

FRANCES: When the pitcher threw the ball, Jane was so proud of herself. She hit it just right and got a home run.

TEACHER: I like "She hit it just right." Who has another idea?

BARBARA W.: The catcher gave the sign for a high ball. The pitcher wound up and threw the ball. Cynthia was so happy because it was the pitch she wanted. She swung with all her might and the ball soared over the fence for a home run.

TEACHER: That's a very good idea.

PAT: When Audrey was going to hit the ball, the catcher said to the boys that she wouldn't hit the ball.

TEACHER: The idea is good, but I don't care for the way you have said it. Try to improve it.

PAT: I will try to make it better.

JAN: After the pitcher wound up, he threw the ball. Shirley swung and hit it. The ball went over the fence. The boys couldn't believe their eyes. She was so excited because she got a home run.

TEACHER: That's better than your first paragraph.

BEVERLY: Then the catcher told the pitcher to give her a low ball. When the pitcher was ready to pitch he made a mistake and threw a perfect strike. Jane hit the ball over the school. She was so happy because the boys would believe that she could play very well.

TEACHER: You have good ideas.

SHARON: Janey was so nervous because if she did not play well she would be out of the game. Finally, it was her turn. She knocked a home run. The boys were speechless. After the game the boys went over to her and told her that she was the only girl that played like a boy.

TEACHER: Let's try writing a story now. Put your two para

graphs together. Be sure to think of a title that will be right for the story. Watch your first and last sentences.

As the children wrote, they were guided in their work if they needed help with spelling, certain verb forms, certain expressions, and paragraphing. Some of them received no help of any kind.

Here are samples of the compositions before major corrections were made.

"LUCKY" SUSAN

One morning Susan was playing with her friends. She played with them all morning. Then she noticed the boys playing baseball. She decided to watch the game because her friends went home for lunch. She came to the boys and asked them if she could play. They said that they didn't want her to play with them. Susan begged them to let her play. They said to her that she could have one chance.

While she was waiting for her turn, the boys giggled and snickered at her. Finally it was her turn to bat. She hoped the pitcher would give her a good pitch. He did. Susan smacked the ball and made a homer. The boys couldn't believe her. They opened their mouths and couldn't say a word. Susan smiled and giggled.—*Marcia*

A PROUD GIRL

One day Susie-Q was playing with her friends on the playground. She was supposed to go home, but she wanted to play with the boys instead. Susie-Q wondered if she could play very well. She ran and asked the boys if she could play with them. They told her that she would have to wait for her turn.

Finally it was her turn. The pitcher wound up and threw a perfect strike. She hit the ball and it went over the fence. The boys couldn't believe their eyes because Susie-Q got a home run. When the game was over, they told her that she could play baseball with them.—*Jan*

A BIG CHANCE

One day Janey saw the boys playing baseball. She went over to the boys and asked them if she could play. The boys told her that she was no good and too young to play. Janey kept brothering them too much. They were disgusted with her.

The boys gave her a chance. Janey was so nervous because if she did not play very well, she would be out of the game. Finally it was her turn. She knocked a homerun. The boys were speechless. After the game the boys went over to her and told her that she was the only girl that played like a boy.—*Sharon*

A BIG SMACK

One day after school Jane was going home and she saw the boys playing baseball. She decided that she wanted to play with them. She walked over to the captain and asked him if she could play with the boys and he said, "No Girls Allowed." Jane pleaded

123

with him and he gave her a chance to play. When it was time for her to play. The boys made fun of her.

The catcher told the pitcher to give her a low ball. When it was time for the pitcher to pitch the ball, he gave her a perfect strike by mistake. She knocked the ball over the school. The boys were so surprised and they opened their mouths and didn't even say a word. Jane cheered up. After the game the boys went over to Jane and told her that from now on they would let her play baseball with them.—*Beverly*

A SOCKER

One day Cynthia was walking by the school field. She saw a group of boys playing baseball. She watched them play. She wanted to play, too, so she went over to the boys and asked them if she could play. The boys laughed. She bragged that she could play well. They snickered at her, but they gave her a chance anyway.

The catcher gave the sign for a high ball to the pitcher. The pitcher wound up and threw the ball. Cynthia was so happy because it was the pitch she wanted. She swung the bat with all her might and the ball soared over the fence for a home-run. She was so happy. The captain was so atishoned that he made her the mascot of the team because she brought lots of luck to the team. —*Barbara*

VERBATIM ACCOUNT OF CORRECTION AND CRITICISM OF STORIES WRITTEN ON THE BLACKBOARD
(taken in shorthand)

TEACHER: First, we are going to talk about all of the stories. I want to tell you something that all of you have done that is not good. When you write a story, you must remember that there are different ways to begin. All of you began your stories exactly the same way. Look. (*Teacher underlined the time phrases in each child's story—"one morning," "one day," "one Saturday afternoon."*) Do you see what I mean? Do you understand? Every girl began her story with "when." (*Teach wrote "when" over the time phrase of every child's story.*) That is one way to begin, but there are many different ways to tell the time of the story. You don't always have to put it at the very beginning of the first sentence. Can you tell your sentence another way, Barbara?

BARBARA W.: When school was out for the afternoon, Cynthia walked by the baseball field. (Original sentence: *One day Cynthia was walking by the school field.*)

TEACHER: That is much better than the other sentence. Can you tell me that idea another way? And don't begin with the word "when."

BARBARA W.: I don't know how.

TEACHER: I think you can make a better sentence.

BARBARA W.: Do you want me to begin a sentence without "when"?

TEACHER: I would like to have you start your sentence without using the word "when" or a time phrase that means "when." Put the time phrase in another part of the sentence. Jan, try to improve yours.

JAN: Susie was playing with her friends on the playground after school. (Original sentence: *One day Susie-Q was playing with her friends on the playground.*)

TEACHER: Come and change it. See the difference? Before, she said "one day" at the very beginning of the sentence. Now she has changed it and she has used "after school" instead. That tells when —it does not always have to be "one day," "one time." "After school" tells *when,* too. This is much better than you did before. How about you, Marcia?

MARCIA: Susan was playing with her friends one morning. (Original sentence: *One morning, Susan was playing with her friends.*)

TEACHER: You have simply moved the time phrase from the beginning to the end of the sentence. That is not very different. That is not very original. Can you do something different?

MARICA: Susan was playing with her friends in the morning.

TEACHER: In the morning? (*Teacher wrote the phrase on the board as dictated by Marcia.*) Do you like "in the morning" and "all morning"? (Marcia had: *Susan was playing with her friends one morning. She played with them all morning.*) Do you like that? You have to think of many different things when you are writing.

MARCIA: I can change it. She was playing with them. . .

TEACHER: Just leave your first sentence and take off "in the morning." Does anybody have another idea?

JAN: Take the first sentence out.

TEACHER: If you take the first sentence out, you spoil the whole story. "She played with her friends all morning. Then she noticed the boys playing baseball." No, you change the whole idea of the story if you take the first sentence out. Do you have another idea?

JAN: No.

TEACHER: Then I would leave it the way Marcia suggested. (*Susan was playing with her friends. She played all morning.*)

TEACHER: Barbara, do you have an idea for an opening sentence?

BARBARA W.: At three o'clock, after school was over. . .

TEACHER: Do you like that?

JAN: Very nice.

SHARON: I was going to say that.

TEACHER: Do you like it? I don't!

SHARON: Why?

TEACHER: It is very long. It is not very interesting. I don't think it is very different. I believe that you can do better than that. Can you improve it?

MARCIA: May I help her? Take "after school was over" off.

TEACHER: That is a good idea. Now it is not so long and it is very different from what you said before. I know another way she could have said it. Does anybody else know?

125

REBA: After school.

TEACHER: Reba says just "after school." Which do you like, Barbara,—it's your story—"three o'clock" or "after school"?

BARBARA: I think "at three o'clock."

(*The discussion continued and the girls suggested many ways of changing the opening sentence to express the idea of "when" differently.*)

TEACHER: We are going to read Barbara's whole story now.

BEVERLY: Why?

TEACHER: Because it is a very good story. She has a good title. She has changed the beginning sentence so that she has a good first sentence. But, there is something the matter with the story. We are going to read it together and I want you to tell me what is wrong with it. Maybe you can figure it out for yourselves. (*Teacher ran her finger under the sentences, pausing at key words while the children read silently. Made suggestion about the sequence of two sentences:* She bragged that she could play. They snickered at her but they gave her a chance. *Barbara suggested the order be reversed. Teacher said to leave the sentences as they had been written.*)

(*Teacher pointed to misspelled word.*) Astonished is supposed to be the word.

BARBARA M.: What does that mean?

TEACHER: Very surprised. Do you know what is wrong with the story? Do you think it is a good story?

JAN: The pitcher gave the signal?

TEACHER: What difference does it make if you say signal or sign? Do you know what is wrong with the rest of the story?

BARBARA W.: I think the last sentence does not belong with the story.

TEACHER: Barbara says the last sentence does not belong with the story. She has a very good idea in the story. She has told many things and she has told them step by step by step and made you excited and then she comes to the end of the story and it falls flat. It doesn't hold your complete attention. The last sentence in the story should leave you with a very good feeling. It finishes the story. It makes the reader have the right feeling about the whole thing. That sentence (*The captain was so atishoned that he made her the mascot of the team because she brought lots of luck to the team.*) does not finish the story in the right way. There are many things that are wrong with it. First of all, it is too long. You have too many ideas. Think of one idea, maybe, or two. Now see if you can improve the closing sentence. Do you all understand the story? You see, she has a wonderful idea. "The pitcher wound up and threw the ball. Cynthia was so happy because it was the pitch she wanted. She swung with all her might and knocked the ball over the fence." She developed suspense and then the whole story falls flat.

JAN: What does "all her might" mean?

TEACHER: All her strength.

MARCIA: What does "soared" mean?

TEACHER: Went high. How would you change the closing sentence, girls?

BARBARA W.: The boys did not believe it. (*Teacher wrote this on the board while the class looked on.*)

TEACHER: Do you like that? (*addressed to class*) That sentence is short but it does not give you the right feeling for the end of the story.

BARBARA W.: I don't know.

TEACHER: Oh, yes, you do.

BARBARA W.: The boys were surprised at her strength.

TEACHER: (*After writing the sentence on the board*) That is related to "swung with all her might." Do you think this is better than the other sentence? It is, but it is not good. (*Teacher circled "surprised."*) That is a weak word.

BARBARA W.: Astonished.

TEACHER: Do you like that?

SHARON: What does that mean?

TEACHER: Very surprised. I explained that before.

JAN: I don't think it's good.

TEACHER: I don't think so either. You can do better than that.

BARBARA W.: The boys watched the ball fly over the fence. (*Teacher wrote this on the board and then pantomimed the manner in which the boys "watched."*)

TEACHER: I don't see that this is very different from "soared over the fence" which you wrote before. You want to be careful not to repeat words because then your story becomes boring.

BARBARA W.: The boys watched the ball going high in the sky.

TEACHER: I don't think that is very exciting.

BARBARA W.: The boys stared at the ball as it disappeared. The boys watched the ball intently as it disappeared.

JAN: That's all.

TEACHER: That's all. Stop right there.

BARBARA W.: I like that better.

TEACHER: That is much better. We could go on and we could make it still better. You must remember when you are writing that the closing sentence is most important. (*Teacher pointed to Marcia's closing sentence.*) She says, "Susan smiled and giggled." It is very, very short for a closing sentence. It tells a lot. She was so happy and proud of herself that she smiled and giggled because she was sort of nervous and happy at the same time. It is a short closing sentence and it is good. There is one other thing I want to tell you about your story, Barbara. Look at this: "She saw a group of boys playing baseball. She watched them playing." Do you need both of those? (*pointing to the two sentences*)

BARBARA W.: No. She watched them playing baseball.

TEACHER: (*Turning to Marcia's story*) Look (*drawing square under "went"*) Do you know what is the matter with that verb? She didn't go home. She stayed on the playground. Her friends went home. Her friends were not there and so she decided to watch the boys play baseball. What happened first? I'm talking about this. (*underscoring "because her friends went home"*) Which happened first?

MARCIA: Her friends went home.

TEACHER: Her friends went home first. Then she decided to watch the boys play baseball. When you put two ideas together and one of them happens first, don't you have to change the verb? Do you know? They have already gone home. I will tell you. When you are telling two things together, and one thing happened first, then you must tell it this way. (*Wrote "had gone" in place of "went"*) because that (*pointing to the earlier event*) happened first. Now look at "came to the boys."

SHARON: She made a mistake. She should say "went."

TEACHER: "Went" is better than "came." Do you know another way to say it?

JAN: She decided to go over.

BEVERLY: She walked over.

TEACHER: She walked over to the boys. "Walked over" is much better than "went." "Came" means to come to me. You come to me but I go to you. She went. Look. (*Pointing to "They said to her that she could have one chance." Teacher crossed out "to her."*) You don't need that. Look. "The boys could not believe her." What would be better to say?

JAN: The boys could not believe their eyes.

TEACHER: That's right, Jan. I think you wrote a good story, Marcia. (*to the class*) She was careful. She had good ideas and I like the way she finished it. I want to show all of you one thing in Beverly's story that is very important and one thing that she must remember. You must be responsible for this. Look (*pointing to incomplete sentence "when it was time for her to play."*) Is that a sentence?

SHARON: She is supposed to put in a comma.

TEACHER: Where? The sentence isn't finished. You put a comma after play, and then you go on and put a period at the end of the sentence. Do you girls understand that? Here you have it. (*pointing to a complete sentence below*) I like that very much. That is good. (*pointing to "by mistake" inserted by child as an afterthought*) You don't say "surprised and." What do you say?

BARBARA W.: Surprised that.

TEACHER: The boys were so surprised that they opened their mouths wide and didn't say a word. (*Beverly had not written "wide."*) I think some of the stories are very good. I think some of your ideas are excellent. Your vocabulary is good. Some of you tried to write so that you had good titles, good opening sentences and good closing sentences. I think the next time you will remember that when you write your first sentence you don't always begin by telling when.

CHAPTER IX

FREEDOM OF EXPRESSION

> Just at the age 'twixt boy and youth,
> When thought is speech, and speech is truth.
>
> Sir Walter Scott
> *Marmion*

THE problem for the teacher of deaf children in their early teens is to keep pace with their rapidly expanding need of language, both oral and written. Their ideas and interests far outdistance their ability in verbal expression. They need so much more than they have as yet acquired, that the teacher is hard pressed for time in which to give them all the language teaching they must have if they are to hold their own in the company of their hearing brothers, sisters and friends.

The compositions of children of 14 or 15 should show an expanding vocabulary and should incorporate a wide range of language principles. Also, the children should put more life, color and individuality into their writing. As an example of what I mean by the last statement I will cite a composition written by a 14-year-old, profoundly deaf girl, child of deaf parents and sister of a deaf boy —a child who has learned the knack of putting herself into everything she writes. Her class was asked to write a paragraph on why they like to read. The composition is exactly as written on page 131.

When asked what kind of books she particularly enjoyed, her written reply was:

Why?? ?????? ?? ????

I like any books especially fiction ~~and~~ I don't know why, but I do. If I am yearning for a book to read, I just grab a book I haven't read and read it.

One more example will show the reasoning and feeling of another congenitally and profoundly deaf girl of 13-and-a-half years of age whose pass I had taken away because of an infringement of rules. The note was written on an ordinary sheet of yellow paper and left on my desk. I am quoting it just as it was written. I have kept the note because I think it is a good example of natural and useful language on the part of a deaf child.

Dear Miss Groht,
    Shirley advised me to tell you that I am sorry I lost my temper and please may I have my pass back as there is only a little while left before school closes and I want to get the best of it before it does. I am bored every afternoon having to stay in while Vera goes out with Josephine. Please let me have my pass back or just for one afternoon. I haven't been in trouble for almost two weeks.

Joan

P.S. And I will try to stay out of trouble.

Language such as this reflects a child's feeling and thinking. It does not follow a pattern set down by a teacher. It is the child's own. Deaf children should express *themselves* when writing, if they are well taught, and they will do so if what they write is interesting and personal to them. A creative teacher will encourage her pupils to write about their personal feelings, reactions and ideas, rather than have them merely report sequential facts and incidents. Even in a more formal type of composition a child's own viewpoint should be manifested.

This type of writing cannot be acquired easily unless a child has, from the preschool on through succeeding grades, been given the language he needs for what he has to say, has learned the real meaning and use of language, has developed an interest in and appreciation of good verbal expression, and has discovered that

Roslyn Jr. Hi II Nov. 4, 1955

Why ???????????????

Why do I like to read? ~~It like to read because~~ I love to read. Sometimes my brain gets hungry and I feed it books. I like to imagine things and I read books to help me imagine better. I hate to sit still, but if I'm reading, I just ~~hate~~ to move or be interrupted ~~interpreted~~ by my brother or the clock.

I love to read because it carries me off somewhere far away where everything is interesting compared with my dull life. When I have no ~~body else~~ but myself to play with, naturally I don't feel like playing. I just grab an easy chair and a good, fat, interesting book, and to be read ~~as I have been saying, books are the best friend of a lonely person who has no one. Here you are~~ So you see, this is my answer to ~~this question.~~ the above

(I'm sorry it's two paragraphs)

Change Closing →

A 13-year-old tells why.

through communication life becomes happier and more satisfying. However, with the right classroom spirit, with children who are alert, eager and interested in things and people, and with an inspiring, enthusiastic, resourceful and stimulating teacher, deaf boys and girls of any age can learn to use good oral and written language. This is true because they will have the right attitude toward it and will find pleasure and help in using it on all occasions. I have seen many pupils move on from the use of prosaic language in their compositions to oral and written work that was exceedingly well done and that gave them and others genuine pleasure.

Subjects for written language should be varied and should have a definite purpose. Plans for excursions, for instance, should not only be discussed orally, but in many instances various responsibilities can be assigned to different members of the class and instructions for carrying them out can be made a lesson in written language. This language would be functional and would have a carry-over into the home life of the children. Along this line might be the writing of plans for an assembly program, giving each child a part in the program; writing captions for posters or pictures; writing labels and information for exhibits; writing directions for tests; writing definitions for words to be used in crossword puzzles; writing directions for playing games; working out rules for a social club; developing the dialogue for a play; writing about interviews held with various people at school or elsewhere; posting notices; writing short messages; and in general using the infinite number of opportunities that present themselves for making use of simple everyday language. To write a terse, clear statement of fact is often more difficult than writing a whole paragraph, and telling a person how to do something is frequently much harder than doing it oneself. All through their lives the deaf will need the ability to write short notes, messages, directions and requests. Because this is so, deaf children should learn how to make themselves understood in a brief, correct and understandable manner.

The writing of news should not be included in the program at this level, although on very special occasions children might wish to tell of a club outing, a family excursion or some very unusual occurrence. The morning conversation period should provide the outlet for making known matters the pupils are thinking about or the things they have done, seen or heard of, or are curious about.

In this department further study of the paragraph should be made. Unless a child knows what makes a good paragraph he cannot write one. If his compositions are to be worthwhile he must be taught how to make them so. In *Speaking and Writing English,* Sheridan, Kleiser and Mathews make the point that teachers often confuse the *act* of composition with the *act of putting down* on paper that which has been composed. One is a *process,* the other is a *product.* Composition is a process of thinking. When a pupil has thought out his three or four sentences or paragraph, the act of composition for him is complete. Yet how many deaf children are given paper and told to sit down and write a story, or news, or other type of composition when they have no ideas to express and are utterly unprepared. The teacher who trains her pupils to think well and talk well will have pupils who can write well.

We have said before that an important point to remember in writing a paragraph is that the subject matter be of interest to the child. It is natural that the more one knows about anything, the more enjoyment he gets out of it. This is also true for English. Children like to write when they know and feel the things about which they are writing. The fact that the topic assigned to a child is of interest to him does not, of course, insure his writing about it in such a way as to interest others. He must be taught to write in an interesting manner. He must learn that what the writer thinks and feels is often of more interest than the bare facts of what he has done or observed.

Children should know by the time they reach the intermediate and upper levels what makes a paragraph a good one. They should by this time have absorbed a paragraph sense. They should know that each paragraph must tell about one facet of the subject, that it should have a topic sentence that will arouse curiosity or expectation, and that the subject should be capable of being developed or expanded. They should be aware also of the importance of the closing sentence. Many well-written paragraphs are spoiled because the writer has gone on writing after his point has been made, or has closed with a flat statement that adds nothing to the paragraph. These points the child should have learned through use, contrast, criticism and praise. A paragraph sense is necessary to effective organization of thought.

The teacher must get the sentence idea and the paragraph idea into the consciousness of the pupils through *use*. She must herself know all the rules underlying the writing of good compositions. Too often teachers lack this knowledge, though it is easily obtainable in the many current books on the language arts. The teacher who prefers drills to compositions will not develop the use of good language in her pupils. Artificial presentation of new language never has and never will bring worthwhile results. All new language given to deaf children must be fraught with meaning for them, must be made clear through associations and experiences. Otherwise the language will be of no use whatsoever to them. This is true from the very beginning of a deaf child's exposure to language. Perhaps an account of an interview with a parent and a child nine-and-a-half years old will show the futility of giving a child language that has no real meaning to him, but that he can memorize and use daily. This child when tested was shown to have an average I.Q. She was friendly and interested in the things around her. Wishing to find out where she stood as to language usage, I gave her paper and pencil and asked her to write what she had done the previous day. It was necessary to show her on a calendar the day I was talking about. The child beamed and started to write. An exact copy of what was on the paper is reproduced here:

News

Today is Thursday .
Yesterday was Wednesday.
Tomorrow will be
Friday

It is Cloudy and Cold
The temperature is
40°,
play doll school
book Car
home florue peter ray

The words at the end of the "weather report" were written when I finally succeeded in getting the child to realize that I wanted to know about her and what she had done—not about the elements.

It is shocking to think that a deaf child could be in a school for more than five years and have so little use of language—and no feeling whatever for it. This child could do a few very simple drills, but could not apply the language principle she was supposed to be learning to anything but the filling in of a few blanks. For her, language was the writing of isolated words, the memorizing of a few sentences.

I do not think for one moment that the case just mentioned is typical, but neither is it an isolated case. I am sure that there are deaf children who are hindered from learning to use English, not because of their lack of ability, but because they have been presented with *language facts* and have had no concept of the meanings behind these facts.

No educator of the deaf has as yet found a cure-all for the present state of the language of the average deaf child, but a few suggestions might be in order. The first of these is that teachers of the deaf do away, once and for all, with regimentation in the teaching of language to the pupils in their classes. If language were an individual thing to each child, it would be bound to have more meaning. Unless it does have meaning, of what use is it to the child?

How make language individual? First of all by insuring that the very young deaf child develop concepts of language through general lipreading involving himself and all his experiences. He should *not,* as we have said before, lipread the names of objects put on a table at a given period each day, "performing" before a circle of little children who do not know what it is all about and who have no particular interest in the objects before them anyhow, since they do not belong to them and in any case will be carefully put out of reach after the lesson. This procedure is no kind of introduction to language. Rather, lipreading should grow through a daily, stimulating contact between children and teachers, children and friends, children and family.

When teen-age pupils use language in a hit-and-miss fashion and have no real basis for the construction of sentences, the results of their writing will be poor. Such pupils are too dependent upon their teachers for correct expression and are unable to think things through because they are not certain of themselves and have no firm basis for using language. Their language is mixed-up, haphazard and indefinite because they have been presented with new language principles when they had neither learned nor understood principles previously presented. It is one thing to *present* a language principle. It is quite another thing to *teach* it. For a student to be introduced to more and more complicated language, when he is unable to handle simple forms or constructions, is merely to confuse him and make his final acquisition of English more difficult.

Before taking up the study of composition, therefore, the teacher of 14-year-old pupils must review all the language forms the children have had and make certain that the children understand the language they are using, or attempting to use. Such review should not take the form of exercises in which children are asked to make up sentences using a particular language principle. Rather they can be asked to write "short short stories" which will naturally call for the use of the form under review. For example, if the teacher is reviewing the use of relative clauses she should not say: "Write a sentence using a relative clause beginning with *who* or *that*." Instead she might say: "I'd like you to write about the person who has helped you most and explain why you chose that person."

It is only when these pupils really comprehend the vocabulary and constructions they need in order to express themselves correctly and interestingly that they are ready to take up the types of writing that children in the upper grades should do. It is well to start pupils off on very short pieces of writing, placing special emphasis on adjectives and verbs because these add much to the interest of the composition.

Little by little the teacher can foster a real interest in language, a feeling for words, a desire for self-expression, an appreciation of good writing. Some groups may not require all this review. If they do not need such reinforcement, they are ready to take up longer pieces of writing, using more complex forms and a broader vocabulary.

More intensive work should be done in the development and use of outlines. Children will produce much better compositions if they have thought out what they are going to say and then put their thoughts in outline form. In addition to this preparatory work they should also consider choice of words, use of idiomatic phrases, and type of sentences they will use. Thus prepared, they ought to be able to write a clear and well-expressed composition.

The work in English at this level should include book reviews, simple biographies, written talks on citizenship, accounts of hobbies

136

and special interests such as stamp collections, art work and athletics, original stories suggested by experiences or pictures, travel stories, imaginary stories, interesting episodes in the lives of various pupils, accounts of newspaper or magazine articles and descriptions of places visited. The pupils should also write letters and notes of all types; they should learn to explain, in writing, why they like to read, enjoy moving pictures, would like to join a club and would like (or not like) to live in the country. Favorite books, games, places and occupations are also good subjects. There are endless ideas for composition, and the teacher should be guided by the particular group she is teaching in making her selections.

An important part of the language program should be the teaching of the condensation of stories, subject matter in social studies, science, reading, magazine and newspaper articles, and reference material from an encyclopedia. Deaf children, just as hearing children, must learn to condense what they read if they are to make use of the material. They must be able to separate the important facts from unimportant detail. They must be able to get the gist of what they read or study, and then express this in a short statement. This ability is essential to the study of any of the content subjects in the upper grades. The child who knows which facts in history, geography, social studies, science and other subjects are most important and are to be remembered, will do far better work and will profit in his studies to a much greater degree than the child who does not know which things are essential and must be learned and remembered.

As a beginning to this work the teacher should start out with paragraphs, putting them on the blackboard and leading the class to decide which are the important points in them. It sometimes clarifies the subject if the important points are underlined in colored chalk. The supporting sentences can be underlined in a different color. Removing the important sentences and putting them down in another space will demonstrate to the class that these tell the story in brief, or designate only the necessary information, while the remaining portions of the paragraph merely add to the essential facts.

Taking sample stories with well-defined incidents, having the pupils decide what is important to the story and what is not, and listing these important points in the form of statements, will show that these statements give the story in the fewest possible words while still keeping it complete in all details. The rest of the story may add to the interest or beauty of expression, and is important for this reason, but unless all the essential points are there the story is not complete. Children must learn to include all necessary facts in everything they write, whether it is an assignment in English or in other content subjects. There are many short stories in readers that can be used for work in condensation. In the beginning it is wise to choose those that have very clear-cut points.

It is often difficult for deaf children to get the main facts of current topics in the newspaper, but this ability should be developed in the grades of the upper school. Far too many deaf people live in a very circumscribed world. Their lives are narrow because they neither read nor understand much that is going on in the world, other than those things that touch their own lives in a personal way. If they are ever to emerge from an inbred social life they will have to become better readers. They will remain unaware of larger horizons unless they can read about them and do so intelligently and with understanding. Because of this circumstance teachers should see to it that their pupils are able to get "the meat" out of what they read both in books *and* newspapers or magazines, and through this process develop an interest in and knowledge of what is going on around them. The newspaper is a very vital adjunct to our daily lives. Being aware of the information and opinions expressed through it is essential for the deaf as well as for the hearing.

If the deaf are to understand and enjoy what they read, they must be able to put themselves into the place of those about whom they are reading. In addition they should be able to visualize persons, places, things and conditions. This is essential not only to the use of reading material but also to the solving of problems in mathematics and to the understanding of facts presented in all the other content subjects. Social studies, for example, will have little meaning for the deaf child unless he has learned to draw a mental picture of what he is reading and studying. The fact that a child can reproduce a topic or paragraph is no sure indication that he knows what it is about or that he understands what he has written. When I first began to teach, a youngster came up to show me a paper she had written in study hall. She said, "I wrote that myself, but I don't understand what it means." There was hope for this child because she *did* want to know what the language meant.

English, as I have already said, is an all-day, continuous subject. It includes so many things that we sometimes lose sight of some of the definite, necessary skills in the mass of material to be covered.

Photo by Norman Crane

Criticism can be friendly.

Conversely we lose sight of the all-around development of the child while working on definite skills. We must bring our pupils to the place where they want to talk and write, have much to talk and write about, and so must have the tools for doing just this. The necessary tools are words—words as they are used in all the various language constructions. Building a useful, enjoyable and valuable vocabulary is a never-ending pursuit. Language comprehension and language expression are closely interwoven. If we teach one we are at the same time teaching the other.

All deaf children whom I have taught have enjoyed any work that has enriched their vocabularies. They have loved acquiring new words. They have been enthusiastic to learn about the choice of words, the different pictures made by changing words, descriptions of the same picture in different language. All these have to do with interpretation of reading and with expression.

For children who have had very little work in word study, the teacher can begin by informally talking about words and getting across to the class the idea of life and color in words. She can make them feel that some words are weak or colorless while others are strong and vivid, and that we can use words and so arrange them that they will make a clear, strong, exciting or beautiful mental picture. This can be illustrated by referring to beauty of expression in poems and prose, for instance, until the children can recognize a graceful, fluent way of saying things when they see it.

Most textbooks on English grammer provide exercises in word study, such as having pupils tell all the words they can think of to describe a given noun. Examples: *water* (clear, blue, sparkling, muddy); or, *soldier* (weary, gallant, courageous). Another exercise is the underlining of words that might best be used to describe a noun: "The house was an *old-fashioned, antique* farmhouse."

Selecting words that are thought most suitable in describing an act or feeling will make pupils aware of the importance of words and awaken them to the knowledge that any old word will not do— that there is a subtle difference in words. The words *fear, terror, fright* and *panic* are good examples. The teacher and pupils should talk about vivid words and the children should learn to feel the difference between *putting* or *shoving* a boat out into the water, or *hitting* or *crashing into* a tree. Children should be made to understand that it is the choice of a word that makes a vivid picture, not the unusual nor the longest word. Seeing mental pictures from words such as *walked, strolled, ambled, dashed, raced, hurried, trotted, galloped* or *ran* is excellent study not only for the use of more interesting English, but also for better comprehension of reading material.

Arranging words in pairs so that each pair will be synonymous and finding synonyms for given words are good exercises for increasing word power.

The teaching of the prefix and suffix is important. Most deaf children learn early the difference between happy and *un*happy, yet falter when they see such a word as *un*comfortable. They were not taught the meaning of the prefix *un,* and therefore are unable to apply it when they see it used in a new situation. By the time they reach the upper school children should know such prefixes as *un, dis, trans, sub, pre, semi* and *inter,* such suffixes as *less, ful* and *able,* and the stems, *port, cent* and others. Forming different parts of speech from the same root—*deceive, deceit, deceitful, deceitfully*— is another valuable exercise.

Teaching *collective* nouns (*crowd, team, family,* used with the singular form of the verb), *abstract* nouns (*curiosity, honesty, selfishness*), and nouns characterizing a person (*coward, stranger, hero, bachelor*), is still another approach to an enlarged vocabulary.

Familiar similes, such as *as blue as the sky, as deep as the ocean, as light as a feather, as cross as a bear* and many others, should be

140

taken up at this time also. Finding "picture words" in a given paragraph or verse of poetry, and underscoring the ones thought very strong or vivid, will help a child to become conscious of the value of well chosen words. For example, the reading with the class of Tennyson's "The Brook" will show how a master can choose words that make an everlasting impression. I have seen many a deaf child delight in seeing words used to convey beautiful thoughts and delightful pictures.

All the work done for building a more comprehensive and interesting vocabulary should be tied up with the *use* of this vocabulary —with expression. Teachers of the deaf should not be content to accept from their pupils, year after year, language that is correct but meager, colorless, uninteresting and trite. Even the deaf pupil himself cannot find value in such language nor be inspired to speak better, write better and read better. Language must have life, meaning, color and importance to the deaf as well as to the hearing.

A set of books which the writer found helpful in vocabulary building is the set entitled *Language for Daily Use*[1], which emphasises the choice of words. Like most textbooks for the hearing, these have much material that is of no use to the teacher of the deaf because her problems in teaching English are not quite the same as are those of the teacher of hearing children, yet the material on vocabulary is very helpful.

Pupils in all grades need constant teaching and continual correcting of question forms. Questions beginning with *how* are often confusing to the deaf. The simplest use is that in which the child asks how a thing is done.

How did John walk? Cautiously.
How did you catch cold? I got my feet wet.
How did Jane cut her finger? With a knife.

Then there is the question:

How do you know that?
I read it in the paper.
Mary told me.
I saw it myself.

Since we seldom use the present participle in replying to a *how* question, I should not teach that form. This would avoid such answers as the following:

How did you hurt your knee? By falling.
How did you catch cold? By getting my feet wet.

---

[1]Dawson, Mildred A., and Others, ed., *Language for Daily Use*. Yonkers-on-Hudson, N. Y.: World Book Company, 1955.

NATURAL LANGUAGE FOR DEAF CHILDREN

Such answers are unnatural and are in poor form. Only when children are familiar with the other responses would I bring in, through reading, such language as, "He got the car rolling by pushing it from behind."

The question form "How long (*does, did*) ————— take to ————?" is always difficult for deaf children because they confuse it with "How long will it take *whom* to ————?" I think that taking short trips, and noting time when leaving and returning, is helpful in establishing a correct concept of these questions:

> How long did it take us to walk to Bloomingdale's and back? 25 minutes.
> How long does it take to fly to Washington? One hour.
> How long will it take you to finish your work? A half hour.

The difficulty with these question forms comes not when a short answer is required, but when a long answer must be given.

"How long did it take Helen to reach Boston?"

The child, unless great care has been taken, is apt to write: "It took Helen to reach Boston four hours." Here is an instance in which the *key* headings might help straighten out the error:

It took *whom how long to do what?*

If the child can remember the order of the words, he can answer correctly. Constant repetition of the correct form is the only way to establish right usage of this or any other question form and this repetition must be obtained, not through unrealistic question and answer drills, but through meaningful experience.

Special verb forms also keep cropping up and need attention— *had to* (I had to finish my work.); *ought to* (Mary ought to help her mother.); *to make* ———— *feel* (The medicine made me feel better.); *make* ———— *cry, laugh, do* (Harry made me laugh.) Idiomatic expressions, such as *to take cold, to take pains, to feel blue,* and verbs followed by like, such as *to feel like, to look like, to taste like, to act like, to smell like,* are also important.

Using connectives often is difficult for the deaf pupil, particularly *for, as, while* and *since, before* and *after.* This is true even though some of the words, when used as prepositions, are perfectly familiar to the child who has long used such phrases as *before school, after church, since recess,* and *for lunch.* As connectives they should be used with the children, both orally and in writing long before they are taken up as a lesson so that, although they are not used by the majority of the class, they are nevertheless not unfamiliar to them. The teacher can accomplish this by giving such directions as: "You may talk quietly to one another *while* I am out of the room." "Don't make a noise *while* you are in the dining room." "Jack has been working on his airplane *ever since* he arrived here this morning." "She was alarmed *for* he had been gone for a long time."

Since is generally used with the present perfect tense when speaking of time extending from some definite point in the past up to the present time. It usually works better if the teacher concentrates on the affirmative in making statements involving the use of *since,* at least for a little while. True statements, such as those listed below, will give the children an understanding of the meaning of the word:

Helen has worn glasses *since* she was ten years old.
Mary has had long hair *since* she was five.
Harold has been in the infirmary *ever since* he fell last week.

In addition to this use, having children answer such questions as the following will give the children an opportunity to use this connective:

How long have you lived with your grandmother? *Since* my mother died.
How long have you taken dancing lessons? *Since* I was a little girl.

Also, the appearance of *since* in conversation, short stories and reading material will further its use by the pupils.

When the children can use *since* in making affirmative statements, I should start them off in the negative form:

I have not seen my grandmother *since* I was a little girl.
Helen hasn't been to the country *since* she was eight years old.

Let children work out their own uses through the telling and writing of real happenings.

The use of the relative pronoun should be given emphasis, for the child should be writing and speaking in longer sentences. As a preliminary to the work with the class the teacher should use these pronouns in schoolroom directions, in stories told or written, and in questions asked. A few examples are:

Please get the books *which* are on the library table.
Give this to the woman *who* is talking to Miss V———.
Will you water the plant *that* is on the window sill?
Once there was a little girl *who* always wore a little red cape.
I'll tell you about a boy *who* was very brave.

Using the pronoun *who* to state some fact which the children know (Miss V——— gave honor badges to the girls *who* used their speech continually.) will make it easier for the children to grasp the significance of the relative pronoun and sense its antecedent.

The children must learn that the relative pronoun *who* tells:

1. **Which person we are talking about—**

Give this to the boy *who* just went down the hall.
or
2. Something more about the person—
Mary saw a man *who* had only one leg.
or
3. What the person does—
A doctor is a man *who* helps sick people.

Children should have practice in giving sentences, such as those given below, to illustrate these rules:

I know a girl *who* can paint very well.
I know a girl *who* has five sisters.
I saw a man *who* was shaking his umbrella at some boys.
A nurse is someone *who* takes care of the sick.

It is always simpler to have the relative clause modify the object in the beginning. Only when the children can use this form correctly would I start having them use the clause to modify the subject (The woman *who gave me this ring* lives near my home.)

Once the children start using relative clauses there will always be some who write long, involved sentences. This should be avoided.

Typical mistakes made by children when using relative clauses are usually caused by faulty presentation and drill combining two simple sentences—a drill that is apt to confuse the deaf child and will not help him know how or when to use a relative clause. Such typical errors are:

1. Awkward expression:
The letter which I wrote my mother I mailed to her.
(Do not accept any sentence which is not expressed naturally or correctly.)
2. A part of the principal clause omitted:
Miss N——— who was our supervisor of speech.
(The use of the Fitzgerald Key will show the child that the main clause is not given.)
3. Using both personal and relative pronoun:
The knife which I found it has a pearl handle.
(Correct by using the Fitzgerald Key, showing two pronouns where only one is needed and pointing out the single antecedent.)

Once the principle of the relative pronoun has been learned, the children should have no difficulty in using all of them—*who, whom, whose, that* and *which*. The children need not learn definitions but should absorb, through use, the fact that relative pronouns connect dependent clauses with main clauses by referring directly to the antecedent in the main clause. The children should understand that the independent clause tells the main thought—the most important thing—and that the relative clause adds more information, just as does an adjective or adjective phrase.

Deaf children enjoy the power of being able to express a thought in more than one way and it should be done at this level, just as in the lower levels. When a new language principle has been added to their fund of language, occasional lessons for variety of expression should be conducted:

We watched a policeman. He was directing traffic.
We watched a policeman who was directing traffic.
We saw a policeman directing traffic.

Each child can choose the sentence he prefers and incorporate it into an account of a walk around the neighborhood.

The important thing for the teacher to bear in mind, as she teaches the more difficult uses of English, is that if deaf children are to progress in the ability to use their mother tongue they must have clear and true concepts of all the language they are using. Children who are interested in writing usually have much to write about and will need constant help in mastering new expressions and more difficult language principles. The child who feels the need for language usually makes known his needs, and the alert teacher will find the way to meet them. She will know *what* to teach and *how* to teach it if her thought is centered on her pupils and their growth mentally as well as academically. The wise teacher will meet all the needs of her pupils, and in doing so will find a co-operative and appreciative response from her class. Teaching language will be happy rewarding labor, not drudgery.

CHAPTER X

BROADER HORIZONS

Style is the dress of thoughts.

PHILIP DORMER STANHOPE,
Earl of Chesterfield
Letters

IN THE second year of upper school the teacher must continue to provide or foster motivation for good writing. Pupils who have reached this level should have a great deal more to talk and write about. To them it is true that, "The world is so full of a number of things." Their writing should reveal enlarged concepts, more abstract thinking, and greater ability to draw meanings from what they see, hear and read. There should be no dearth of ideas—no hesitancy in self-expression, no lack of participation in discussions, either individually or in class. The writing should also show a greater awareness of social factors, particularly as they affect teenagers. There should be greater spoken and written social communication, not merely between the child and adults but between the child and other children . In fact, lack of language should no longer be a barrier to more realistic thinking and acting.

These pupils should now be ready to forge ahead in the use of English in much the same way that hearing boys and girls of 15 and 16 use it, though the teacher will still find it necessary to correct mistakes in language constantly and to strive to improve the written work of her class in order to make it more effective. These pupils should be able to revise their own writing and improve it.

Continued emphasis must be placed on the use of connected language in such activities as personal conversations, discussions, and written compositions and in talk about the subject matter of the curriculum, entertainment projects, special programs, the planning of school functions, and in all types of correspondence.

Many of the suggestions for original work given in the preceding chapter would also be applicable in the area now under discussion. Perhaps it would be well to provide added impetus to writing in a more imaginative vein by giving pupils an opportunity to sharpen

146

their thinking along original lines. One class at Lexington School wrote an imaginary conversation between an elephant and a donkey that figured in the news around election time. One of the results of this kind of writing follows:

WHAT A PAIR!

"I know curiosity killed the cat, but I just can't figure what kind of an animal you are," a donkey said to his fellow traveler on an airplane bound for the U.S.A.

"Well," the fellow traveler answered cooly, "if you must know, I'm an elephant, and please don't gape at me as if you had never seen a long nose before!"

"Oh, I'm sorry; I didn't mean to," the donkey said, trying to be friendly, "I'm Judy from Saudi Arabia, and I'm on my way to the U.S.A. as a gift to Ike's grandson from King Saud's son, . . ."

The elephant interrupted, forgetting the insulting look, "And I'm Danny. I am an African elephant, bound for the National Zoo of the U.S. Say, how did you get caught?"

"What do you mean?" the donkey said with a questioning look.

"You mean that you have never been a free donkey. I mean, haven't you ever roamed around in the jungles freely, and suddenly found yourself in a man-smelling trap? That's how I was caught. I hate all men and their foul odors!"

"Don't you say that about all men," retorted the donkey, "all of them are not like that; I was treated like King Saud himself in his Royal Zoo!"

"Do you expect me to swallow that stuff?" sneered Danny.

"Look here, Danny. Every word is true! Did all the elephants in your crowd have the same type of personality?" Judy asked.

"Err, well, no," Danny answered.

"Well!" Judy said triumphantly, "That is the same way with men, and the kindest of men are zoo keepers."

"Gee," exclaimed Danny, "I hope that is true because I am going to a zoo."

At this point, the airplane whirred to a stop, "Oh, it's time to get off. Judy, please get David to bring you to visit me in the zoo! I guess I'll be with the other elephants. And I hope what you said about zoo keepers is true. Bye!" said Danny hurriedly.

"O.K. Bye, bye," called Judy over her shoulder as she was being led down the plank by serious faced men.

A dialogue between a cat and a dog, given as pets to a child and offered a home by him, would bring out original thinking also. Newspapers frequently run photographs of strange or bizarre incidents and these often intrigue the children. They enjoy writing about how they think the illustrations might possibly be interpreted. Along this line is the writing of a simple fable. Describing cartoons and giving personal reactions to them also enables the children in the upper classes to express personal opinions and assumptions.

Writing captions for pictures stimulates children to strive for apt expression of ideas and moods.

The following are illustrations of captions written by some of the upper school pupils:

Under a picture showing a silhouette of a working man, pipe in mouth, tools underarm, a student wrote, "Here comes Mr. Nobody."

For a picture showing great masses of clouds drifting above a forest, another pupil wrote, "Over earth and ocean with gentle motion."

Another child caught the feeling of movement in a picture of a little girl strutting briskly behind her Tabby cat by writing, "Halt! March one, two, three, four!"

This type of writing calls for a different use of language from that ordinarily used in composition. Whether the expression be humorous, poetic or just charming, a few choice words are needed to capture the predominant feeling that the picture evokes.

Creative writing, that into which the child puts all he thinks and feels, is the highest type of composition for him. Through it he reveals himself and his basic interests and needs. I have seen many a child change from a withdrawn, inarticulate and unresponsive person to one who felt secure, happy and accepted, once he was able to express himself through creative writing. He was awakened to a knowledge of himself, and this resulted in his inclusion into the life about him—first in the schoolroom and then gradually outside it. He felt great satisfaction in what he wrote and was pleased when others liked his efforts. Language for him became indeed a blessing.

The writing of humorous stories and funny incidents is an excellent form of composition for the deaf. To see humor in a situation, and to convey it either orally or in writing, is often difficult for deaf children. Yet once they can do this both their conversation and their written work will take on new interest. Being able to incorporate a bit of humor in friendly letters is also an asset to deaf and hearing correspondence alike. The following postscript appeared at the end of a letter a pupil wrote to her teacher during the summer vacation: "P.S. I hope you will not make me work too hard when I return to school. I feel very lazy! ! ! !"

Deaf teenagers are no different from their hearing counterparts in their need to learn the language of "tact" for both speaking and writing. Many a deaf boy or girl has been rebuffed by a teacher or some friend, not because of the matter broached, but because of the language used in doing so. There is a great deal of difference between saying to an adult: "We want you to chaperone us to the party." "You must take us to the party," and saying: "We would like it very much if you could chaperone us to the party." "Can you do us a favor? Would you take us to the party? We would appreciate it."

Many little acts of courtesy are neglected by deaf children because they do not have the language to clothe their real feelings. There is a language of acceptable behavior and deaf children must be taught this special language. To express sympathy or understanding, and to make offers of help or encouragement, requires a knowledge of the right thing to say in any and every circumstance. It is too often demonstrated by the deaf that though they perceive the subleties of human relationships and respond to the deep needs of others, and are not at all insensitive to other people's suffering, grief, trouble and conflict, they do not have the language with which to express their feelings. This lack puts them at a grave disadvantage, and they are often thought not to care about others. Actually they seem unable to give comfort or condolence because they just don't know how to express their innermost feelings.

It is an important part of the teacher's work to help her pupils develop ability in the use of this type of self-expression. This cannot be done by providing model letters and having children follow them in writing letters to imaginary people, because such notes or letters should express genuinely sincere and personal feelings of sympathy and thoughtfulness. Therefore, the teacher should have pupils respond to actual situations whenever they arise.

The notes that follow were received by members of the staff at Lexington and are simple illustrations of this type of writing.

> 904 Lexington Avenue
> New York City 21
> November 20, ——

Dear ————,

We were surprised on Monday when Mrs. W———— told us about your mother's death. We want to express our sympathy to you on your loss.

We hope that we can help you when you return to school.

> Love,

> ————————————

> 904 Lexington Avenue
> New York City 21
> October 1, ——

Dear ————,

I heard that you were very ill. I am really very sorry. I hope you are well now so that you can come back to school. I have been thinking about you because I want you to get well and also I like you very much.

Love,

—————————

904 Lexington Avenue
New York City 21
October 1, ———

Dear ————,

The Book Week Assembly was very successful, but it would have been better if you had been there. I was very nervous up there on the stage, and I needed your smile of approval to spur me on.

Sincerely yours,

—————————

Again, in more happy situations, deaf teenagers who have learned how to be pleasant, thoughtful hosts or hostesses are apt to be the ones who have the most satisfactory social lives and who are never ill at ease when in gatherings of either hearing or deaf people. These are the deaf children who have learned how to greet guests, put them at their ease and see that they become acquainted with one another; who can start a conversation when that seems necessary; who can say the correct thing when serving guests. Poise is as attractive in a teen-age deaf boy or girl as it is in a hearing boy or girl.

I should like to clarify one thought in the matter of social grace. Deaf girls who are taught merely to serve food correctly at a tea or other function, who know how to carry a cup of tea to a guest, are not necessarily well-trained in social manners. It is what they *say,* even more than what they *do,* that labels them as socially adequate and properly trained.

Many a deaf boy or girl has learned how to respond to others in exactly the same way as do their hearing brothers and sisters. Deaf children have individuality, personality and charm which they reflect constantly in their contacts with other people. Just as the hearing young person colors his speech with the use of colloquialisms, so can the deaf. An apt use of an idiom or common expression can lighten or make vivid a remark by a deaf child. As an illustration, a 16-year-old girl with no measurable hearing, having been given charge of arranging an assembly program, replied to the teacher who asked what she was planning, "I think I'll talk to Miss ————'s class about the matter and see what they come up with."

Deaf children of all ages *can* use colloquial English in just the way that hearing children do, spontaneously and to the point, provided they have been taught the use of language as a way of looking at things. They can use current and popular expressions as a handle for pleasant interchange of remarks in ordinary conversation. Deaf children who can do this find themselves on an even footing, not only with hearing contemporaries, but with hearing adults.

The following expressions were garnered during one day by some of the teachers whom I asked to keep track of some of the incidental remarks and expressions used by their pupils. The pupils were not aware that their expressions were being collected:

I knew what you wanted. *I read your mind.*
I don't know what you're saying because I *can't see through* Mr. C———.
We had a *little something* to eat.
Treading on dangerous ground means that you're putting yourself *on the spot.*
I begged her for a long time and she finally *gave in* and said I could have the ballet shoes.
I got soaked to the skin.
That's too *wordy.* You can use one word to take the place of so many words.

Another aspect of language teaching is helping the deaf to accept ideas and beliefs that differ from their own so that they may be able, through thoughtful discussion, to see and appreciate another's point of view. The deaf who have a circumscribed understanding and use of language frequently find it hard to be open-minded about opinions at variance with their own. It is not only a part of the teacher's work to provide the right language for happy, integrated living on the part of the deaf, it is her sacred duty to do so. Deaf boys and girls do not stay in school forever and they do not have a teacher always beside them. While they are in school it is important that they have the experience of discussing amicably their opinions on different subjects, ranging from their favorite ball team to current political issues.

Other language teaching at this time should cover needs for learning to say things effectively in correct English. To succeed in getting new ideas across to other people, one must be able to speak in such a way that his remarks will have the desired effect. The deaf child who has something definite to impart to another person needs the language that will state the information clearly and concisely. He needs words that will be persuasive and perhaps intriguing, and above all *clear* to the listener. Should he be unsuccessful in having his ideas accepted, he needs the right words with which to accept defeat gracefully. One of the best ways to get this sort of language over to the child is to have classroom discussions on current subjects, or to have interclass meetings, parent-pupil talks, and sessions with hearing teenagers from other schools. Class discussion in preparation for meetings with other groups should be an important part of the language program in the upper school.

We read the following in *Language Arts for Today's Children*:

> Growth in ability to communicate is also an essential part of the development of the self. The child who learns to communicate with ease and satisfaction tends to build up an outgoing personality and a friendly relationship to others; whereas the one who is retarded in his language development or finds his efforts to communicate frustrated may become timid or inhibited or may turn aggressive and strike out at the world.[1]

Again, in the same book, these wise words may be found:

> The child's growth in language is closely bound up with the development of his own personality. In an age of increasing pressures and tensions, he needs especially warm interpersonal relationships with other children and with adults. The emotional tone of his life is expressed through the communication essential to ordinary everyday living. Conversation, and, in much smaller degree, letter-writing are the basic language activities through which these interpersonal relationships are achieved.[2]

The teacher of the deaf should see that her pupils can, and do, discuss both objectively and subjectively all those happenings and conditions that touch their lives day-by-day. This ability can be acquired by the deaf as it is by the hearing, if the foundation is laid in the early grades.

As in the lower grades, so on into the upper levels it is imperative for the teacher to talk about those things her pupils are studying so that she may ascertain what this study has meant to them, whether or not their concepts of the material are correct, what *they* think about the things they have supposedly learned, and what value or importance they put on such information. In content studies children should not be giving back the exact wording of the textbooks, but rather should be putting the information into their own language. What the deaf pupil reads or studies is of value to him only as it broadens or affects his thinking, his behavior, or his way of life.

Throughout all the work in composition there must be constant vigilance as to correctness of the language used, for in the upper

---

[1]National Council of Teachers of English, Commission on the English Curriculum, *Language Arts for Today's Children*. New York: Appleton-Century-Croft, 1954, p. 20.

[2]*Ibid.*, p. 4-5.

grades the very volume of material requires knowledge of difficult language forms. Teachers indeed have a problem in trying to discover how to give the boys and girls in the upper classes the ability to use all the language principles they need in order to express themselves adequately and correctly. No teacher, however fine an instructor she may be, can ever give her pupils all the forms of all the principles they must know. The best she can do is to teach each and every pupil to reason, to think things through, to make his own deductions, to apply new knowledge to old and to associate old knowledge with new. This can be done if the deaf are taught *principles* of language and not merely *facts*. Having been writing articles on the teaching of language to the deaf for more than 25 years, and stressing the futility of having deaf children spend hours of school time on teacher-made drills with no direct relation to the child and his needs, I was pleased to read what Ruth Strickland had to say on the subject of drill:

> Drill has a place but it tends to be successful only when it is purposeful practice in a skill which the child understands and for which he sees some practical need. Superimposed drill with the motivation stemming from teacher requirement is rarely fruitful of secure and permanent learning regardless of the number of repetitions involved. Practice, in which the motivation stems largely from the child's desire to acquire the skill to serve his purposes, may be highly valuable. The stronger the child's inner motivation the fewer repetitions he will require for mastery.[3]

There has always been, in schools for the hearing as well as in schools for the deaf, a wide divergence of opinion as to the value of a systematic course of teaching grammar to elementary school children. As long ago as 1896 Dr. Davidson, of the Pennsylvania School in Mt. Airy, wrote:

> As there are always a number of our pupils preparing for higher schools which require an entrance examination in technical grammar, we are obliged to teach this subject in our more advanced grades. Although I know a few children of a peculiar mentality to have been greatly benefited by the study, ordinarily I do not consider it of much value in the teaching of English, so no more time is given it than is absolutely necessary.[4]

What, then, are teachers of the deaf to do about grammar? If studies of the value of teaching grammar to hearing pupils have

---

[3]Strickland, Ruth, *Language Arts in the Elementary School.* Boston: D. C. Heath and Co., c1957, p. 329.

[4]Davidson, Dr. Samuel G., "Advanced Work in Language and Literature with Oral Classes," *Report of the Proceedings of the Fifth Summer Meeting of the American Association to Promote the Teaching of Speech to the Deaf.* Washington, D. C.: The Association, July 1896, p. 143.

proved that it is of little or no value to the natural language usage of these pupils, will the deaf find more help by learning definitions, parsing words, analyzing sentences? I think not! In the chapters on the lower school the matter of having deaf children absorb grammatical facts through their usage was discussed; for example, the use of the period, question mark, comma and capital letter. These were added in the lower school as the child grew in his need of such facts. They were not learned through definition or rote. So in the upper classes, pupils should be taught grammatical facts as they have a need for them. The correct use of language must be stressed, but again not through formal definition.

Let us see what modern educators have to say on the subject of teaching grammar in the elementary schools. In *Children and the Language Arts* Dr. Esther J. Swenson says: "Analysis of language with attendant emphasis on structural detail should follow rather than precede the child's grasp of the meaningful whole."[5]

In the same book Dr. Lois Gadd Nemec and Dr. Robert C. Pooley have this to say:

> Children learn the use of language long before there is any need for them to analyze its structure. Therefore, in the elementary grades the major emphasis will be upon the actual use of language and the improvement of skills through use, rather than upon knowledge about the language itself and attention to restrictive rules. In curriculum terms the foregoing generalization would indicate that grammar of the analytical and structural sort will have little or no place in the elementary grades, but that the oral and written conventions of English, those which function in actual speaking and writing, will be of chief concern.[6]

Again these educators reach the following conclusions from observations and research:

> Time spent upon formal grammar in the elementary grades is time taken from the practice of skills in the speaking and writing of English. . . . For the grade school child, the skills in the use of English greatly outweigh knowledge about the English language. Even the future utility of grammatical terminology is insufficient justification for the use of limited time to teach structural analysis of English. Concentration upon the actual use of English in all the kinds of situations which an active life and a rich curriculum make significant for communication seems unquestionably the first task in English teaching of the elementary school.[7]

---

[5]Herrick, V. & Jacobs, L., ed., *Children and the Language Arts.* New York: Prentice-Hall, Inc., 1955, p. 443.
[6]*Ibid.,* p. 289.
[7]*Ibid.,* p. 298.

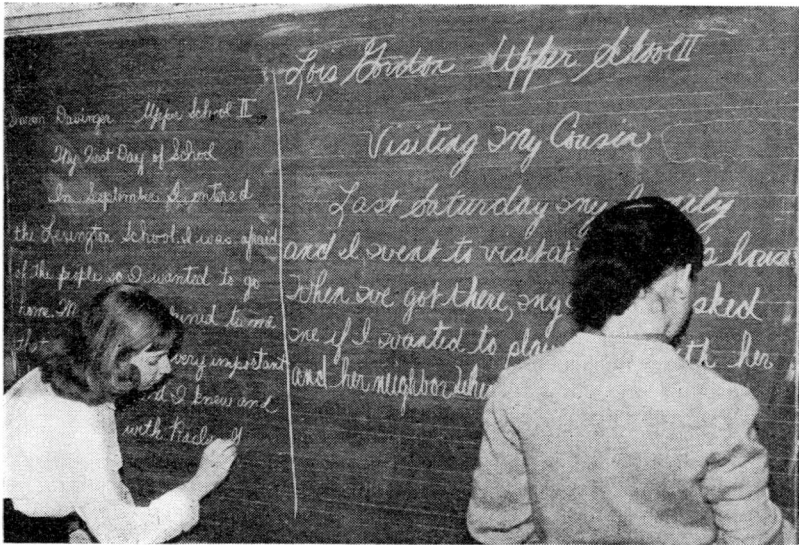

Photo by Norman Crane

Our language is individual.

The deaf child, even more than the hearing child must have continual practice in the *use* of English. All his waking days he should be learning correct English—in school and out of school, through communication, through study and through reading. All the language he learns in the schoolroom should be part and parcel of him outside the classroom. All language work involves the use of grammar and every teacher should have a comprehensive knowledge of it. She should know how to give to her pupils the ability to use correct English by multiplying instances of its use. There must be constant reminder and effectual explanation on the part of the teacher, incentive for remembering on the part of the pupil, and above all there must be repetition in meaningful usage.

Pupils in the higher grades should know how to look up language forms in the dictionary in order to find out for themselves what the particular tense of a new verb should be. They should know how to use a reference book, encyclopedia or textbook. They should learn language from the books they read and should be able to store in their minds those language forms and expressions that will be useful to them. A deaf child in his teens, if he is "language conscious," will gain knowledge of the use of language from reading, just as a hearing child gains knowledge of the use of language through his hearing.

155

NATURAL LANGUAGE FOR DEAF CHILDREN

If deaf boys and girls are to grow in the use and understanding of language when they have finished school, they must be fortified *while in school* with the ability to learn "on their own." Learning is a never-ending process, for the deaf no less than for the hearing, and this applies to the learning of language. The amount of language a deaf child has when he leaves school will not be sufficient for him ten years later. He must by then have acquired a greater command of English in order to be successful in his work and in his social life. If he is to know what is going on in the world and understand what he reads in newspapers, magazines and books, he must constantly improve his understanding of English. Textbooks and school library books are necessary, but to read beyond these is an even greater necessity. Therefore, the teacher must constantly keep uppermost in her mind the thought that she must make her pupils good readers, not just for the time they are in school but for all time. She must make them aware of the importance of language not only for speaking and writing, but for comprehension. Keeping this broad view of the value of and need for language always before her, the teacher will find ways and means to give to her deaf pupils the desire and ability to keep using and improving their knowledge of language.

CHAPTER XI

ON THEIR OWN

The object of teaching a child is to enable him to get along without his teacher.

ELBERT HUBBARD

STUDENTS in the last two years of school are nearing graduation, and they must be prepared to meet the challenges that will come to them. Whether they are preparing for a higher education or for making a living in the business world, their success will depend to a large extent upon their acceptable use and understanding of English.

How should we prepare these boys and girls for the challenge that awaits them? The answer is that we must anticipate their needs and provide them with the knowledge and ability to meet all requirements through a clear, correct and encompassing use of language. We must teach them how to think through the mass of reading material that will be given them, how to evaluate such material and separate the important from the unimportant facts, how to make outlines for garnered information. We must train them to be objective about what they read or study, to be clear and concise in expressing themselves and to be objective in reporting on their reading and study. All these things they must do by themselves, and they should be fortified through language to do so before they leave the school for the deaf.

Pupils who reach this level have been "through the mill" when it comes to the acquisition of the basic skills in written and spoken English. They have by now established a pattern of communication which should enable them to understand others and to express themselves in clear and correct English. Their need now will be for new and better forms of expression and an appreciation of the value and enjoyment to be found in good writing; for an

157

Photo by Norman Crane

Conversation comes naturally to teenagers.

enlarged and enriched vocabulary; for correctness of expression; for a use of figurative language to express deep feeling, beauty and longing.

To be sure these pupils will need guidance in the intricacies of construction, but this should come through daily discussions of the language they are using in their written work. Their comprehension of language should be of such a broad nature that they can absorb, through understanding and assimilation rather than the doing of exercises, new ways of saying or writing what they have in mind. They should have by this time a real sense of responsibility for the kind of language they are using and should show a definite interest in perfecting their own use of English. They should know their good points and their weaknesses.

Having had guidance in their writing for years, they should now be showing an individuality in their mode of expressing themselves; they should have a style all their own and their writing should reflect themselves. Self-expression should be the keynote. There should be more independence of thought as well as independence of expression. The compositions at this time should be more than just well-written. They should have an appeal for the reader because of their content, the manner in which ideas are presented, the use made of idiomatic or current expressions, the choice of colorful or very apt words or phrases, and the over-all interest of the subject.

Pupils in these classes will show wide individual differences in their use of language. The gifted children will be more creative in expressing their thoughts. There will be originality in all they write and often a genuine sparkle in the vocabulary selected. On the other hand the more prosaic writer will need guidance in making his work more interesting and in giving it an appeal to the one who will read it.

I submit, as an example of individualistic writing the following uncorrected and unsolicited writing of a girl, nearly fifteen, who indicates no response to sound. This "essay" was handed to her teacher one morning!

ME AND MYSELF

I am an average girl; there is nothing special or terrible about me. I have a younger brother who is a brat, typical of what many girls have. I like boys and like to go out like anybody else. I plan to go to college, get a career, then settle down, like the majority of high schoolers would. I am a poor speller, but being good at algebra makes up for it. My English is average, and I read just about the same number of books the other girls read. I have the typical American looks;—brown eyes and brown hair. I don't think I should go on writing as you know all about me. I am just like any other girl you know.

This girl has her own style and anyone knowing her could select her writing from a group of compositions. There is a definite flair to whatever she says or writes. Individuality in language can be fostered and nurtured. The person who develops his own style is better understood and appreciated and invites from others a more personal interest and contact.

One of the ways in which to help children establish their own styles of writing is by first developing in them an appreciation of the distinctiveness of the writing of the authors they are studying. There ought to be a close tie between the language and the literature programs so that one enhances the other, and yet each contributes toward the children's understanding of what constitutes good writing.

Some activities for developing this feeling are:

(1) Studying authors—learning about their personal lives and the world in which they lived, trying to see how these things were reflected in their books. The children should now be able to think along with others and follow their thoughts and ideas.

(2) Listing many verbs in one category and examining the subtle differences in meaning as, for example. the verb *to look*—*watch,*

peer, peep, see, glance, notice, stare, gape, gaze, spy, sight, spot, catch a glimpse, observe, focus.

(3) Listing adjectives under the five senses as, for example, the sense of touch—*soft, hard, smooth, rough, uneven, slippery, sticky, bumpy, satiny, silky, velvety, prickly, fuzzy, hairy, spiny.*

(4) Collecting picture words such as *mammoth, wee, delicate, fragile, dejected, broken-hearted,* and figures of speech such as *floating on air, up in the clouds, fits like a glove.*

(5) Finding different expressions for the same idea—*at crack of dawn, bright and early, up with the sun.*

(6) Studying idiomatic expressions involving multiple meanings for a single word—*take a train, take cold, take a walk, take turns, take care, take pride in, take advantage of, take issue with.*

Such activities will give children a love for really good language and will help and inspire them to improve their own writing.

Creative writing is rather difficult for some deaf pupils, but surprisingly enough it is less difficult than expository writing. If my readers have ever had the experience of following directions for playing a game, making a "do it yourself" article or filling in forms from given directions, they will realize how difficult it is for anyone to give clear and concise directions. Exposition is difficult even under simple conditions because it requires the recognition of the important as against the unimportant, and the ability to arrange these facts in a logical and uncomplicated order.

On occasion any deaf person will have a need to write to someone, giving him directions for reaching some particular place, or finding a certain shop, or making a complicated trip, or negotiating a business contract, or transacting business of one kind or another. How, then, can the teacher prepare her pupils for such use of English? First of all she can do this by giving many and varied opportunities for the use of exposition in the classroom. Examples of such assignments might be:

Giving directions for getting to one's home
Giving directions for taking trips
Giving descriptions of how things were made or done
Describing buildings or monuments
Explaining procedures for routines in libraries, offices, etc.
Giving instructions in sewing, swimming, cooking, etc.
Describing such things as the American flag, the state flag, the United Nations flag
Writing about the U.N., the Bill of Rights
Writing about the duties of the President of the U.S., the Vice-President, the Supreme Court, Congress
Telling how books are made, newspapers printed
Explaining membership in a book club
Giving opinions on current happenings

Explaining games or sports—baseball, golf, skiing
Discussing customs of other lands
Relating the origin of various national holidays
Examples of expository writing by deaf pupils will be given at
the end of this chapter.

In order to cover the many language needs of the pupils at the
Lexington School many suggestions are taken from textbooks. The
Bailey and Lewis Series have been found to be particularly helpful
in the upper grades.

Supplementary texts used in English in the Upper School classes
are:

Adventures in English—Burleson
Allyn & Bacon, N. Y. 1939
English First Course—Stoddard, Bailey and Lewis
American Book Co., N. Y. 1948
English Is Our Language—Sterling, Lindahl and Koch
D. C. Heath & Co., Boston, Mass. 1950
Language for Daily Use—Dawson, Miller and Zollinger
World Book Co., Yonkers-on-Hudson, N. Y. 1955

The work in language is not confined to these books, since the
deaf have many problems in language usage that are not covered
by books written for the hearing. On the contrary the deaf have
no need for exercises on such uses as *seen* for *saw*, *ain't* for *isn't*,
double negatives and the like.

At this point I should like to submit a verbatim account of a
lesson given by Mrs. Margaret Wood to a class of five girls in the
tenth grade. Four of these girls entered our school at nursery age;
the fifth graduated from a public school for the deaf about three
years ago and has been with us ever since. The youngest girl,
Roslyn, is not yet 15; the others are 16, except Florence, who is the
girl who came to us three years ago. The lesson was taken down
as it took place and no corrections have been made.

This is one of the best ways of showing what actually transpires
in a classroom where you have both an inspired teacher and a receptive group of youngsters. It will be worthwhile to notice how
skillfully the teacher directs but does not dominate the discussion,
and how the ideas emerge from the children and are given most
appropriate expression through the collective efforts of the group.

TEACHER'S AIM

To guide the class in developing good opening and closing
sentences.

MOTIVATION

Dr. Groht is writing a book, as you know, and she would like
to include one of our lessons. I have selected several topics that I

161

think you would be interested in discussing. Let's choose the one you find most interesting.

1. The value of an education.
2. English is a necessary subject.
3. The value of lipreading and speech for the deaf.

(After discussing the topics, the girls decided on "English is a Necessary Subject.")

TEACHER: That's a good choice. Why do you think English is a necessary subject in our schools?

ROSLYN: The majority of Americans speak English.

ANNA MARIE: It is necessary to know English in order to get along with Americans.

ROSLYN: English plays a part in everyday life.

TEACHER: That's a good idea.

FLORENCE: If the students have a good English background, they can understand better.

TEACHER: Understand what?

ELAINE: Their work.

TEACHER: That's much better.

ANNA MARIE: In order to be able to read, write and speak, a good English background is necessary.

ROSLYN: Another word for "necessary" is "essential."

TEACHER: Use either necessary or essential. Carol, you seem to have an idea.

CAROL: If it wasn't for the English Language, we wouldn't be able to understand or communicate with others.

FLORENCE: The American students should have a good English foundation so that they can get along with and understand their work.

TEACHER: That's similar to what you said before.

ELAINE: It is difficult for anyone to understand a person who has poor English.

TEACHER: It *is* difficult to understand people with poor English, but we try to understand them.

ROSLYN: Everything in school has English as a basis.

TEACHER: Good. That's true.

ANNA MARIE: Understanding the English language helps us understand our work.

TEACHER: The idea is good, but we have said it before in another way.

ROSLYN: English is a means of communication among us. A person must have fluent English if he expects to make good in America.

TEACHER: All of you have given many good reasons why English is necessary in our schools. Let us try to develop a good topic sentence for each paragraph now that you have some ideas to work with. What is a topic sentence?

ANNA MARIE: A topic sentence contains the main idea of a paragraph.

TEACHER: Right. Have any of you ideas for topic sentences?

162

CAROL: To obtain a good education students must be capable of doing excellent work in English.

TEACHER: That is a long and rather awkward sentence. See if you can improve it.

CAROL: May I think about it for a few minutes?

ANNA MARIE: English is a necessary subject in English-speaking countries.

TEACHER: I don't care for the last part of the sentence. It sounds repetitive.

ANNA MARIE: In all American schools.

TEACHER: That's better.

ROSLYN: English plays a big part in everyday life; thus it is an important subject in American schools.

TEACHER: That's pretty good. Elaine have you thought of an opening sentence?

ELAINE: English is a part of every school subject.

TEACHER: That's true. That's all we have time for now. Be thinking of other topic sentences before class tomorrow.

SECOND DAY

TEACHER: Yesterday you all gave good reasons to show that English is a necessary subject. Today we want to compose good topic sentences. Be sure that your sentences are not too long. Make sure that each sentence is to the point and contains the principal idea of the paragraph.

ANNA MARIE: English is an important subject in everyday life.

TEACHER: I don't care for the phrase "in everyday life."

ANNA MARIE: How about in school work?

TEACHER: That's better.

ROSLYN: How about in schools?

TEACHER: Let Anna Marie choose the phrase she likes better.

ANNA MARIE: I prefer "in our schools."

TEACHER: Florence, have you decided on a topic sentence?

FLORENCE: American students who have good English can do their advanced work better in school.

ANNA MARIE: It's too long.

ROSLYN: She has a good idea. But it's confused.

ELAINE: It's okay, but she can improve it.

ROSLYN: It's awkward.

CAROL: It could be more catchy.

ANNA MARIE: She has a good idea, but she didn't put it right.

ELAINE: I agree with the girls, but she can fix it up.

ROSLYN: How about—American students who have good English can do more advanced work better than those who have poor English.

ANNA MARIE: That doesn't sound like you. There are too many words.

CAROL: It's too wordy.

TEACHER: I agree with both of you. I also think she can express the idea more clearly. Do you think you can help her, Anna Marie?

163

ANNA MARIE: Good English will help American students understand their advanced work more easily.

ROSLYN: That's a better sentence, but I don't think it is a good topic sentence.

ELAINE: She's right. It's better for a closing sentence. How about this—Acquiring fundamental principles of English is necessary for everyone.

TEACHER: The beginning is excellent, but I think *everyone* is a poor word.

ROSLYN: How about *every student?*

TEACHER: That would be better.

ROSLYN: The acquisition and daily use of good English are what every student is trying to get.

TEACHER: I don't like the last part of the sentence.

ROSLYN: I agree with you. How is this—With the daily use of good English the student can help improve himself.

ELAINE: Advance himself sounds better to me. What do you think of—The acquisition and daily use of good English are what American students need to improve themselves.

ROSLYN: That's what I mean.

TEACHER: That's a good topic sentence.

ANNA MARIE: It's simple but good.

TEACHER: It is to the point. Carol, what's your topic sentence?

CAROL: English is a required subject in most schools.

ROSLYN: I like—The most important basic subject in school is English.

TEACHER: You have done better with your topic sentences today. Be thinking of good closing sentences for the next lesson.

THIRD DAY

TEACHER: We are going to develop closing sentences today. Remember that a closing sentence must bring the paragraph to a good conclusion. It provides the finishing touch and leaves the reader with the right impression. It pulls the whole paragraph together. What have you decided to use or suggest as a closing?

FLORENCE: We have written to improve the American student's English. I'm afraid that's clumsy and wordy.

ROSLYN: She's confused.

ELAINE: The language is not good.

ANNA MARIE: It doesn't make sense. May I give one?

TEACHER: All right.

ANNA MARIE: For these reasons it is true that a good understanding of English is necessary in all American schools.

TEACHER: That's pretty good.

ROSLYN: For the above reasons English is a necessary subject in school.

TEACHER: It's not bad. But I think you can do better. Try to improve it or make another one.

CAROL: These are the reasons why English is essential in school programs.

TEACHER: That's all right.

164

ELAINE: Learning the necessary principles of English gives the students a better understanding of their work or *improves* students' work or *makes* the students understand their work more easily.

ANNA MARIE: Learning the necessary principles of English helps the students broaden their knowledge of other subjects.

TEACHER: I think it's rather long.

ANNA MARIE: To have a broad field of knowledge, English is necessary.

FLORENCE: To give American students a better English background is a good idea.

TEACHER: It is much better than your other sentence.

ROSLYN: For people to attain their goals in life, English is an essential.

TEACHER: That's much better than your other sentence.

ELAINE: These facts prove that English is the most necessary of all subjects.

TEACHER: Good.

FLORENCE: What would students do without English? or, Students would not be able to get along without English.

FOURTH DAY

TEACHER: Now we are ready to write the paragraphs. Be sure to open with the topic sentence that you decided was the best. Arrange your reasons in good order. Then finish it with your best closing sentence. Be sure to have an appropriate title. *Remember* your topic sentence determines the person and tense that you will use in your writing.

(These are some of the paragraphs that the girls wrote. They have not been corrected.)

THE IMPORTANCE OF ENGLISH

English plays a big part in everyday American life, thus it is a basic subject in our schools. If the students have a good foundation of English, they'd be able to go through their school work and additional work much faster. Many jobs require good use of this subject. For the student who wants to attain success, English is an essential.—*Roslyn*

ENGLISH IS NECESSARY

English is a necessary subject in our schools. It helps all students have better understanding in their other subjects. It is part of their everyday life wherever they go and whatever they do. It is a means of communication in speaking, reading and writing. For these reasons it is true that English is an important subject in all American schools.—*Anna Marie*

ENGLISH AS AN ESSENTIAL

Acquiring the fundamental principles of English is essential for every student. It helps him understand his work more easily if he has a good foundation in speaking, writing and reading. If he has ability to use good English, he has less trouble in his school. He uses it daily everywhere in society, school and work. These facts prove that English is the most necessary of all subjects.—*Elaine*

The above lesson shows plainly, I believe, that deaf pupils can hold classroom discussions as well as hearing students. These periods are enjoyed by the pupils, who are completely relaxed and vitally interested. They speak their minds when in disagreement, but always in a friendly spirit of cooperation.

It seems to me that the type of work done in this class can best be shown by giving some of the subjects for compositions and by including some of the work of the class.

Describing buildings in school neighborhood:
    The Police Station
    The Manhattan House (new apartment building)
    The Polish Embassy
    The New York Foundling Home
    Hunter College
My First Day at "904"
An Interesting Event
Stories of all kinds:
    Suggested by pictures in the news
    Imaginative
    Humorous
    Personal
My First Date
This Cold War
New Year Aims

In addition to the above type of work, students in their last year of school should be able to do the following without error:

Give and take messages.
Report conversations they have had with others.
Summarize talks and discussions.
Write editorials.
Answer questionnaires.
Write proper applications for jobs.
Know how, through correct use of language, to handle difficult or awkward situations.
Have a usable knowledge of grammar.

In fact, they should have such a complete and useful use of language that they will never be at a disadvantage in their contacts with hearing people.

Language to these pupils should be a living, enjoyable and satisfying way of dealing with circumstances that are necessary, personal and self-satisfying.

EXAMPLES OF COMPOSITION

WHAT A DATE!

There was nothing exciting, romantic, or different about my first date. It was just a plain old date. It all began in November 1956, when Arnie asked me for a movie date scheduled for a month later. With much hesitation, I finally accepted.

When that day came, he was about an hour too early, and as the dining room is next to the living room, he watched me eat a full-course dinner all by myself. At last we got to Times Square, and we went into the first theatre we saw.

My curfew was 11:30-12:00 A.M., so we planned to catch the 11:25 train; thus we would be home a few minutes before midnight. We missed that train by a few minutes because I thought that it was not polite to run. We had to wait an hour for the 12:25 train, and I opened my door to meet Mom's serious face at 1:00 A.M. Luckily, she was understanding, but she warned me about the next time, and let it go at that.

I never went to a movie with him again!

THE REPORT CARD

During dinner, the subject of report cards came up. "Oh, Mommy, that reminds me," Little Nancy said as she was getting up. "Mine came today, and I'll go get it."

Soon she was back, clutching that report card tightly in her little hands. "Mom, here is my January report card," she whispered.

It was so quiet that you could hear a pin drop as it was passed around for the older members of the family to look at. Mom's stern voice broke the dreary silence, "Nancy McGowan, what happened??"

"Oh, oh, oh, oh well, Mom," she stammered nervously, pulling an excuse out of thin air. "Well, you know, everything is marked down after Christmas!"

904 Lexington Avenue
New York 21, New York
September 20, 1957

Dear Miss Chute,

Mrs. Wood and my class were discussing your ability as a writer, and your style of writing. I realized fully what she meant after I read the captivating story, "The Blue Cup." I felt that I just had to read the whole book, and I nearly did before my time was up.

I want to thank you very much for sending a first edition of *The Blue Cup* to the Lexington Library.

Sincerely yours,

VOTING

Voting is a privilege and a duty. That goes for every citizen who is over the voting age and he should appreciate this precious thing. He is entitled to that privilege and he can vote for whomever he pleases. If he recognizes voting as a duty and has high

167

ideals about democracy, he would vote in every election. He should get out and try to convince other people to vote if he wants the country to be well-governed. If he is really thankful for what he has in this country, he would do all his duties.

AN OPINION

The suggestions of changing all national holidays to Monday is a ridiculous idea. Why, if I were the president of the United States, I wouldn't do such a thing as that. The people should know better before they say anything because holidays are a tradition and they are supposed to stay where they are. Secondly, the dates of famous events will be all mingled up and how are the students to know the exact dates? Thirdly, the number of accidents will zoom quickly because of the long weekends. And last of all, business will drop because so many employees have long days off. If Congress is on the verge of passing this suggestion, I would not waste any time because I would gather a group of people who disagree with this idea to help to influence them not to pass the law.

THE POLICE STATION

The dull red brick building is one of the most important buildings in the neighborhood. There are two large windows, one on the left side and the other on the right side on the main floor. There are six windows grouped in two's on the next three floors. There is a tower with three windows on top of the building. The large entrance is between the two large windows and there are two funny-looking lamps on the wall on either side of the door. The dirty black gates are along the first side of the building. Our large American flag hangs on the second floor. There is an annex on each side of the building.

| | # A WILL—AND A WAY

The best way out is always through.

ROBERT FROST
A Servant to Servants

IT HAS been suggested to me by more than one teacher, in schools using a formal and analytical approach to the teaching of language, that I include in this book some hints and suggestions that would be of help to them in an effort to change the system in use to one where the natural method is used.

To make this change, there must first of all be a desire for the change and a consciousness of the need for it. I should like to emphasize the fact that the entire staff must be willing to cooperate in the venture, for the change must be made from the lowest to the highest class if satisfactory results are to be achieved. I have taught teachers for many years and in many places. They have always indicated a feeling that the method they were following was inadequate. They have wanted to change the pattern of language teaching, but did not know how to begin. It can be done! But the wheels of change turn slowly.

It might be well, at this time, to mention one point which has been called to my attention on several occasions. I have always used the natural method of teaching language to the deaf. I have seen it used successfully by literally hundreds of other teachers through the years. Even today I am sometimes told that only an exceptional teacher can follow the natural method without becoming hopelessly lost. I do not believe this. Any teacher who is willing to read and study the teaching of language to hearing children, to spend time watching the acquisition of the first language of little children, and to adapt that knowledge to the teaching of the deaf—can follow the natural method. If such a person is the exceptional teacher, then I stand corrected. But I do not believe that the average teacher of the deaf prefers to suppress her imagination and limit her teaching to cut-and-dried lessons outlined years and years ago. It is my opinion that most teachers who follow this practice do so because it was what they were taught to do.

Those who wish to change to the natural method may benefit by some of my experiences at Lexington School. I will not attempt to include details about the teaching techniques. Many of these have been incorporated in the various chapters of this book. I will, however, try to give a general idea of the way we went about changing from one method to another.

When I first came to the Lexington School it was following the the same plan used by most schools for the deaf in those days. Great dependence was placed upon a series of language books based on the analytical approach. The exercises on language principles were stereotyped and did not represent ideas of the children. Ready-made sentences were the order of the day. All the children had to do was to insert a proper verb, pronoun, adjective, etc.

Conjugation of verbs was used to give knowledge of tenses. Questions and answers were based on stories or sentences. All of this took a great deal of time. The teachers did not have to be creative. They did not have to really think about language—what it was and what it should do for the child. They had each day's lesson cut out for them. There were also textbooks on question forms and on the use of direct and indirect discourse—again, language unrelated to the child.

Since I had received my training in a small private school for the deaf where none of these books were in evidence, and since I had taught for several summers at the Davidson School of Individual Instruction at Tamworth, N. H., I honestly did not understand these methods. I could not see how they helped the deaf child to use language naturally, as did all the hearing children I knew. All my life I had had hearing babies and little children around me. I knew children and how they learned first to understand and then to use language, step by step in a happy, useful way. Then during my training I had seen deaf children who could be talked to as if they could hear—who could respond when spoken to, even though this was not always done in perfect English. In that school it was taken for granted that children would watch a speaker's face and try to understand what was being said and would respond.

At Lexington School I was fortunate in having Dr. Harris Taylor for a superintendent and Miss Edith Buell for a supervising teacher. Both of these educators were farseeing, progressive and receptive to new ideas. They were willing to let me teach my way and were interested in the various approaches I used. Like many others at that time, however, they were not sure that all teachers could get results from such an informal program even though they believed in it wholeheartedly.

During those first years at Lexington School I followed my method and the rest of the school continued to use the textbooks for the deaf, though with a gradual loosening of method. The language used by the pupils was correct, but limited.

When Dr. Taylor appointed me supervising teacher 25 years ago, I think he did so because he had confidence in what I was doing. It was the kind of teaching he believed in, and he wanted to give me an opportunity to demonstrate the method beyond my own class.

It is not easy to change a method that has long been in use. It cannot be done overnight. The users of the old books had to have time to change their thinking and their approach to language. Many of them had been following the analytical method long before I had become a teacher. There were doubts to be overcome, but the teachers were cooperative and the school administrators had faith in the natural method.

To start with, I did away with all the outdated books. I suggested that teachers cut out the pictures from the old books, which they did. Since both pupils and teachers had long been in the habit of having the same picture used and the same story learned about it, my first step was to give the children identical pictures, but they were allowed to give the characters names of their own choosing. This made for individuality at once—for each child chose a name he liked. Then each child told his own story about the picture. The idea pleased everyone and before long the children were revealing that actually they *did* have ideas of their own and that they loved what they had written.

After all the pictures had been used, I introduced pictures from little reading books where each child still had a picture which was the same as those of all the other children. This I continued to do in order to show that different people have different ideas about what they see. Later, using pictures from magazines, each child wrote a story about a picture that was unlike any others and was of his own selection.

In those days teachers had long been accustomed to teaching certain language principles at certain times. Because there were so many innovations in the language work, I allowed teachers to continue to stress some particular language principle each week, but I insisted that it be taught by means of natural circumstances and never through the use of stereotyped, meaningless drills.

We stopped the conjugation of verbs, and the children no longer had to learn all the forms of each verb at one time. *Needed* tenses were stressed continually.

Emphasis was placed on oral English—conversation, storytelling and guessing games. We tried making oral English a definite part of the daily curriculum. To be sure, the children had always had many opportunities for giving replies when spoken to, for asking and answering questions and for talking in speech periods, but we wanted more than this. We wanted them to *converse* and to do so naturally and adequately.

We began this work in classes where the children were in their fourth year of school. These were pupils who had entered school at the ages of five and six. The teacher, on a rainy day, would tell the children what *she* did on rainy days and perhaps what she did on rainy days when she was a little girl. Then she gave such opening phrases as, "When it rains ————," or "On rainy days ————," and would have the children tell what they did on such days. A few samples will illustrate:

> When it rains I don't go outdoors. I stay home and play with my doll.
> On rainy days I dress up in my cowboy suit. I pretend I'm Tom Mix.

The same idea was worked out one bright sunny day, the opening phrases this time being, "On sunshiny days ————," "When the sun shines ————." Examples of children's remarks follow:

> On sunshiny days I skate with Bobby. I can skate very fast.
> On sunshiny days I wheel my doll up and down the street.
> When the sun shines I play outdoors.

Other popular beginnings were, "When I was very small ————," "When I was a little boy ————," or "When I grow up ————," for the children enjoyed telling about themselves. Examples: "When I grow up I will be a doctor and take care of sick people." "When I grow up I'll drive a car. I will not drive very fast." The boys in particular showed great relish in telling of pranks. There was a great difference in the remarks. One should not expect all children to be alike in their use of language because some have more interesting ideas than others. Where one child writes, "When I was very small, I sucked my thumb," another will write, "When I was a little boy I put a lot of toothpaste on a doorknob. My mother put her hand on the knob. She was very cross with me."

Topics for oral English were drawn from the children's experience—"What I Saw," "What I Found," "Where I Went," "What I Made," "Visiting Grandma," "Sick in Bed," "A Wonderful Surprise."

In the fifth- and sixth-year classes the pupils talked about what they had seen or done at home—what character they liked in a book and why—what they expected to do during a vacation—what their favorite season was and why it was the favorite—what they had enjoyed most at the circus, a show or a party.

Sometimes they told about members of their families:

When my mother was a young girl she was a nurse in Russia. She wears earrings in memory of her mother.

My mother was born in New York City about 1897. Her father is living but her mother is dead.

Once the teachers grasped the technique they proved that they were not lacking in ingenuity. Their ideas were endless—and the children responded!

The pupils in the upper grades used the oral English period for discussing books and giving out information on various subjects. They sometimes had topics assigned about which they were to talk. No pupil got up to talk unless he was prepared to do so unhesitatingly, willingly, and in a manner interesting to his hearers. Occasionally some idiom was assigned which had to be incorporated into the talk given. This quite often led to interesting narration, as the following talks by some eighth-year pupils show.

One day I lost a hairpin. I looked on the floor, on the bed and on the chair. I hunted *high and low* without success. "Henny" helped me and at last she found it in my locker.

Once I lost my ring. I searched *high and low* and could find no trace of it. Suddenly I saw a sparkle under the sofa. I realized it was the stone in my ring. I was glad to have it again.

"Oh, where is my puppy?" my little cousin wailed. "Don't worry, I'll find it," I said. I searched *high and low* but no trace of the puppy could I find. At last I remembered the closets— and in the first one I saw the puppy fast asleep in a corner.

The children delighted in having odd and funny incidents told to them. A few of them quite often prefaced their remarks with, "This is very funny," or "You'll laugh at this."

Sometimes the pupils thought out what they wished to talk about in study time and jotted down what they intended to say. Sometimes they asked the teacher to look at what they had written for possible correction in language or for help in pronunciation. The slip of paper was used for reference, should the speaker find such need. Gradually the teachers saw less and less reference to papers and eventually no need for them at all.

After the children had much practice in "telling things" or in talking to the members of the class, they were encouraged to broaden their experience. If sufficient interest is aroused, children can be inspired to repeat what has been said. Teachers sometimes suggested, "That's interesting. Wouldn't you like to tell that to Miss N.? She'd laugh, I think," or "Let's ask Miss C's class to come up and some of you may tell them about our trip," or, "Be sure to tell that to your father when you go home."

Within a year the children were talking a great deal more than ever before. They held conversations with many people—not just their teachers and classmates. They liked to communicate. They had gained confidence in expressing themselves. Because their oral language had become more interesting, more fluent and more correct, their written work improved immeasurably. Language became a living thing.

When children have learned what can be done through language, when they see in it not only knowledge but pleasure and satisfaction, they have the incentive to further their use of it. The children did not want to revert to the old method of memorizing, filling in blanks or doing any of the so-called language drills. They wanted to speak and write about all those things that touched them personally, interested them keenly and gave them great satisfaction. As the announcer says when speaking of the *New York Times,* "It is much more interesting and you will be, too." This applied equally to Lexington pupils.

The custom of having deaf pupils memorize and reproduce corrected language was discarded from the beginning. News items, stories and all types of written work were corrected and discussed. All errors were carefully explained. Common class errors in language were noted and these principles were retaught, no matter in what grade they appeared. It was agreed that a deaf child must *understand* the language he is trying to use, for only then will it become his. Attempting to use language not fully understood is the basic reason for the use of poor English by the deaf.

"Action work" for the teaching of prepositions, verbs and pronouns was discontinued. These language principles were learned by providing meaningful experiences in which their use was demanded. Through written news and short stories and through reading materials, pictures, conversation, storytelling and games, the correct use of such principles was established. We used "toy stories" (see Chapter V). The ability to ask and answer pertinent questions was developed in natural circumstances. The habit of answering questions about stories or news items was stopped. Answering questions on facts already known was also discontinued, as was the giving of a short and a long answer to a single question. The children soon recognized that usually "short" answers are given in oral situations and communications, and "long" answers more frequently in written work. The various question forms were taken up when natural circumstances warranted this. For needed repetition in their use, the teachers planned additional, but natural circumstances and activities. Deaf children need to ask questions when they want to know something. Questions that arose during the course of the day were the ones stressed and these were always used when called for.

In changing from a traditional to the natural method there are sometimes intangibles to be overcome. I remember that when the transition to the natural method was put into practice at our school, some of the older pupils felt that the teacher was not doing her job because she was not giving them a great deal of written work on drills. They did not understand so much informal conversation, were not aware that they were learning new language during informal talks. I well remember taking over a class when the teacher was ill. I had looked over her plan and had seen that she had planned to work on relative clauses and certain verbs that were to be used with them. When the pupils came in they were surprised to have me for their teacher, but were nevertheless pleased to see me. One or two of the girls said, "May we talk for a while?" (Deaf children love to sit and talk at any time.) We spent the fifty minutes having a fine time chatting about all sorts of things. Next day, the teacher was back and the children said to her, "Miss Groht took your place yesterday, but she didn't teach us anything. We just talked and had a marvelous time." Actually we had done a lot of work on relative clauses.

Again I recall that when Miss Buell moved me from the intermediate department to the advanced department, where I had five classes in English every day, it took a little while before the children began to see what the change from stereotyped work to original work meant to them. Once they were conscious of the fact that they were using language that was *theirs,* and that made for broadening and interesting experiences with others, they showed assurance and initiative in both oral and written work. They learned that having a good vocabulary was an asset both in and out of school, that words were wonderful things and the better the word in oral or written work, the better the effect on those who heard or read.

Those pupils who had latent gifts for expression were, within a few years, able to do better than average work in composition. They possessed a large and illuminating vocabulary and could express themselves in an original and interesting manner. This increased use of language was channeled into the writing of worthwhile and interesting letters. The following write-up of a lesson in English, which was demonstrated in 1933 at The International Congress on Education of the Deaf, will show clearly what the natural approach to the teaching of language to the deaf can do. The compositions were to be based on an unpleasant experience. A general outline was given. The first day the subject was announced. The pupils discussed possible titles for their own compositions—"A Narrow Escape," "Locked in a Classroom," "Lost in the Woods." The children then suggested possible situations, some of which were:

1. You started to explore a deserted house.
2. You wandered off into the woods.
3. You were walking along a lonely street.
4. You came upon a deserted island.

The next step was to work out a possible vocabulary, and lists of good words and phrases were made. A few examples are:

ignored—paid no attention to—disregarded

pleaded with—begged of—appealed to

persisted in—kept on with—continued to

despised—held in contempt—had only contempt for

I would like to add here that these pupils had for some time been making lists of "little phrasings" in individual notebooks. These were resorted to in the same manner in which words were looked up in a dictionary. "Little phrasings" was a method for enriching the vocabulary, devised by the authors of *New Method in Composition*.[1]

The second day the teacher told *her* story of an unpleasant experience she had had, using in her narrative as many "picture words," "telling words" and "little phrasings" as were necessary for an interesting and clear account of what had happened. As each useful word appeared, a pupil put it on the blackboard. I will give the story as told by the teacher, underlining the words

---

[1]Boylan, William A.; Fuller, Constance W.; and Taylor, Albert S., *New Method in Composition*. New York: Charles Scribner's Sons, c1934. (o.p.)

which the boys and girls had written on the board. The story was taken from the lips and given but once.

Most of the family had gone out for the evening, but my sister and I, having had a *strenuous* day, decided to remain at camp. Everything went well for a while and then, *without warning,* there were steps on the *porch* outside our windows. Immediately we *regretted* having stayed at home. *To the best of my ability* I hid my fear and *exerted* myself *to calm* my sister who was *in a panic.* When the door knob was turned, I *trembled with fear* in spite of my efforts. Fortunately the door had been bolted. A knock! I *ignored* it but whoever was outside *persisted.* My heart stood still! I *cautioned* my sister to remain quiet. I *despised* myself for being afraid, yet was unable to answer the knock. Then a face *appeared* at the window. To my great surprise it was only a young girl. I *reluctantly* opened the door and admitted her, though I was *still suspicious.* We soon found our fears were *ungrounded,* for the girl was in *greater terror* than we. She was a stranger to the neighborhood and had lost her way. When she saw our light she naturally hastened toward it.

You may be sure it was with great *relief* we found our fears were *unwarranted* and we *firmly resolved* never again to become so easily terrified.

After the list of words and phrases had been put on the blackboard, the pupils placed beside each word or phrase another that might have been used in its stead, thus giving a wider choice of words. For example:

strenuous—hard—difficult
immediately—at once—at that moment
regretted—was sorry—repented
trembled with fear—shook with fright
cautioned—warned
to the best of my ability—as best I could

The teacher's story having been told, the pupils were ready to discuss theirs. Topic sentences were suggested and written on the slate. A few were: "Nothing will ever again frighten me so much as an experience I had one night last week." "One day last spring I found myself on a deserted road in Westchester County." "As soon as John and I stepped inside the door of the haunted house our troubles began."

After this discussion the pupils went to the blackboard and wrote their compositions, bringing into play the words they had chosen as most fitting for their stories. It being a class of pupils who had been doing the same sort of composition work for a few years, they had no difficulty in selecting good words and phrases and it was unanimously agreed by the visitors that the results were surprisingly good. This, however, did not deter the pupils when it came to the third step, which was the *revision* of the compositions. The stories having been read by all, each pupil undertook to revise another pupil's story, making changes in the vocabulary or phrasing, inserting idiomatic expressions, reversing constructions or taking out unnecessary sentences. This sometimes necessitated consulting the original writer as to his exact idea, and these revisions were carried on in a very cooperative and understanding spirit. After the revisions were made, a class discussion took place as to whether or not the changes had improved the original story and why. In some instances it was decided that the revision had immeasurably improved the story. In other instances it was agreed that the changes had made little difference, while in still others the new words were not so good as those used by the original writer. In all this work in paragraph study, the children showed a very friendly, cooperative spirit and an intense interest and pleasure, each one most decidedly looking and aiming for betterment in composition and appreciating suggestions not only from the teacher but from his classmates.

The wording and phrasing having been settled to the satisfaction of all, the following class comment and criticism took place. The pupils looked at each beginning and asked such questions as: "Does it arouse interest?" "Does it give an idea of what is to follow?" "Does something happen in it?" "Does it state a fact that the rest of the paragraph proves?"

Next, the story was discussed and these questions considered: "Is there a point to it?" "Does the writer stick to the point?" "Does each sentence help to unfold the story?" "Are there any unnecessary details?" "Are there any picture words?" "Are there any especially good ones?" "Are there too many of them?" "Are there any unnecessary sentences?" "Could you omit one?" "What sentences are particularly good?" "Has the writer put his own feeling into his story?"

Lastly, the ending was discussed: "Does it clinch the point of the story?" "Does it tell what the writer thinks and feels about the incident?"

The reader will have discovered by this time that the boys and girls were doing actual paragraph study and doing it in an able way. Yet of what use would this ability be if it could not be applied in a more definite way and linked to the life of the child? The answer is," "Of no use," so the following day the next step was taken up and formed the desired link. This was done by having the pupils write to a relative or friend telling about the unpleasant experience, employing the same or similar vocabulary as that of the composition. Before the children went to the blackboard to write their letters, the teacher read them a letter she had written to a friend, telling of her unpleasant experience. If the reader will look back at the teacher's story, he will see the close connection and the use of the language in each instance. The letter follows:

July 15, 1932
At Camp

Helen dear,

You will laugh when I tell you of a very *funny experience* I had one evening last week, though at the time, it was *extremely unpleasant.*

Mary and I were alone in the house for we had had a *difficult* day and had not wished to join the others on a trip to the village. We were *comfortably settled* in the library, each with an *absorbing story.* Everything was *serene* for a while and then we were *startled* to hear steps on the porch. At the sound, we were sorry that we had remained at home. I covered my fright as well *as I could* and *attempted* to *assure* Mary that all was well. In *utter fright* she had crouched behind father's big arm chair. I was *badly frightened* myself and to try *to calm* her was like the blind leading the blind. *Suddenly* the door knob rattled! Then a knock! *I shook with terror* until I *remembered* that *through good fortune* the door was *latched.* We must have had an unconscious *premonition* for as a general thing, the door was left unlocked. After a few breathless moments, there was another knock. I *paid no attention* to it, but the person outside *kept on.* I *warned* Mary to keep very still. I *hated* myself for being so *petrified,* yet could not bring myself to go to that door. After a moment's silence, which seemed like eternity, a face was pressed against the windowpane. To my *untold amazement* it was the face of a young girl! I then *hesitatingly admitted* her though I was still *apprehensive.* It was not long however, before we realized our fears had been *unwarranted* for the girl had been far more *frightened* than we. It seemed she was a *newcomer* in the neighborhood and *had wandered* from the beaten path. Seeing our light, she had sped toward it, hoping to find *assistance.* Can't you picture us heaving one big sigh of relief when we found our *terror* had been *uncalled* for? We have made up our minds that in the future it would be *wiser* to *investigate* matters before giving ourselves up to *imaginary* fears.

Not all our experiences at camp have been unpleasant. We have had, on the contrary, more pleasant than unpleasant times. Daily dips in the lake, picnics in delightful spots, hikes through the woods and many other such agreeable activities fill our days. When I see you, I shall tell you about them in more detail.

Give my love to the family—the big as well as the little ones.
Love to you, too,

M——————

As with the story, so with the letter. The pupils listed on the blackboard the words and phrases which they thought were best and later wrote, beside each word, another of the same meaning. It will be observed that the letter carried the same thought as the composition. The pupils, in their letters, sometimes used the exact wording of their revised compositions, but more often than not they preferred a synonym or similar phrase. In the letters a personal note was always added. If pupils are interested and alert, they will find no obstacles in the way of expression and will enjoy building up a discriminating vocabulary. Also, they will hold *themselves* responsible for their own improvement, which is the greatest step that can be taken. In the class about which I am writing, it was no unusual thing to hear such statements as these: "When I wrote my composition I used a different expression, but I like this better." "I made a mistake in the use of that verb last Monday, but I know the right use now." "The other day I wrote the past perfect but today I wrote the past. It's better."

It is often amazing to the teacher to find that the children, without referring to finished work, will know just exactly what they did or did not do, and therefore assiduously avoid repeating the error. All that is necessary is the proper attitude toward their work.

Since all this work was done on the blackboard so that the visitors could observe, I am unable to show the excellent compositions of the children. That the use of the natural method had been of value was demonstrated, however, by the achievements of the pupils.

Compositions about accidents, surprises, outings, inventions and an infinite variety of subjects furnished the basis for interesting and varied compositions and the foundations for rich and entertaining letters. A pupil, who had worked out a composition about a practical joke, used the knowledge gained in correspondence with her family to produce one of the most amusing and fascinating letters I have ever read. Real writing, not doing exercises, paid great **dividends.**

Even the language worked out in business letters was often utilized in a practical way. It had always seemed to me a most uninteresting procedure to have pupils write isolated business letters, principally because it was a requirement and had to be included in the year's work. On the other hand, by creating occasions for the letters, the procedure assumed a different aspect! There were always occasions to be found for writing letters for information, such as asking for pamphlets, for passes to visit a steamship or an exhibition, for detailed information about trips and the like, but it was not always so simple a matter to find interesting occasions for applying for positions, ordering and exchanging goods, making adjustments and notes of that kind.

In a class of wide-awake boys and girls much was accomplished in the form of games or by bringing the imagination into play. The following program gives a fair example of the method we followed in approaching the usually cut-and-dried matter of writing letters, ordering goods, and taking up the adjustments so often necessary in straightening out the incidents frequently connected with such activities. The teacher, having in mind this objective, wrote notes to the children inviting them to spend part of the Christmas holidays at her camp in the mountains. She made a point of telling each one to be sure to bring ice skates, skis and a warm leather jacket. The children, upon receipt of the notes, entered heartily into the play. In the discussion of the invitations it naturally was discovered that John had no skis, Mary did not own a warm jacket, William had no ice skates, and others lacked sundry necessities. The logical thing to do next was to pretend to order the desired articles, and the letters were accordingly written to the stores decided upon by the pupils. It was interesting to note that the boys chose stores well known for sporting goods, while the girls selected department stores with which they were familiar. The children then wrote acceptances to their invitations, explaining that they had ordered the things the teacher said were needed. The next step was full of possibilities! John's skis were supposedly received, but they were too small and had to be returned. William received his skates, but his gloves did not come. Mary's jacket came, but it was not the right size and color. All sorts of adjustments had to be made. What a wealth of material for the writing of business letters, and what fun to do it! In due course of time everything was satisfactorily settled, and a day was set aside in which to act out the visit. That it was a happy visit goes without saying! Then letters were written to friends telling all about the fun in the mountains.

There are endless ways of securing practice in writing business letters. One very good game is to allow the boys in the class to represent the business houses and reply to letters written by the girls; or the girls might pretend to be secretaries for the business houses and thus have the duty of answering the letters sent in. Any teacher having a genuine interest in stimulating the children in her class will find it easy to go on indefinitely creating possible situations. It is as true now, as it was then, that teachers must use their ingenuity to create situations which make for language learning. When real situations arise, however, the pupils can handle them.

In letters of application, the language used can be carried out in personal letters. In one class the writer told her pupils of a friend who had moved to the country and who wished to find a young girl to be a "mother's helper" and to assist with her two small children. The friend also wanted a boy to help with the outside work —cut the grass, weed the garden and do whatever chores would naturally befall a boy in that capacity. The pupils talked about the necessary requisites for filling such positions. The girls decided they should really be fond of children, be able to sew and mend, be successful in entertaining and amusing children, know how to care for them and, since the house was near a lake, know how to swim. The boys felt that they should be willing and industrious, like gardening, love the out-of-doors and be generally useful. One enterprising boy decided to write that he had had experience painting shutters, putting up screens and mending fences. Letters were then dispatched. In order to make further use of the language learned, the pupils later wrote letters to their mothers, telling what they had done and repeating what qualifications they had given as to their fitness for the positions. One pupil wrote:

Dear Mother,
    You will never guess what I did yesterday so I shall have to tell you! I wrote to a friend of Miss ———, applying for a position as mother's helper during the summer vacation. I told the friend that I had had experience taking care of children. (I was thinking about the many times I have taken care of little John.) I wrote that I was very fond of children and had always been successful in amusing them. I also said that I liked to make children's clothes and could mend and darn neatly. The family live near a lake so I mentioned the fact that I was a good swimmer. Don't you think that will make the mother feel that the children will be safe with me? I did not want to tell her that I was only fifteen, but my teacher thought that I ought to state my age. I am so tall that most people think I am eighteen. As soon as I receive a reply to my letter, I will let you know whether I receive the position. Aren't you proud that your daughter is growing up and will soon be able to help you?

Everything is going well at school. Today we are all busy writing letters. It's lots of fun.

Write to me soon. Love to the family.

Your loving daughter,
Edith

All the language of the letters of application was used in this natural and spontaneous manner and thus became living language for the child. Unless language *is* carried over in this way, the child will not make it part of his daily thought.

The above lessons have been given in detail because first of all they demonstrate that it is not necessary to limit the deaf child of average ability to the use of a limited vocabulary and an uninteresting and stultifying use of language. He does not have to speak and write "like a deaf person." The deaf can acquire a natural and desirable use of language just as can a hearing person. Some people do better in expressing themselves than others. This is true for both the deaf and the hearing, and in both instances it is true that **the finer the teacher and the better the home environment, the** finer the results. In my opinion the natural method has been more successful than methods where language is presented and taught too analytically and with little attention to individualities, innate abilities and rewarding outcomes.

The end results for those who have been taught by the natural method have been a greater and stronger desire to communicate, a keener interest in self-expression, an increasing ability to write well, and a greater resort to the reading of books and other materials for pleasure and self-improvement. Results over the years have been gratifying, not only to the children, but to all who have come in contact with them.

APPENDIX

SUGGESTED BIBLIOGRAPHY FOR TEACHING LANGUAGE

Artley, A. Sterl (chairman), et al., *Interrelationships Among the Language Arts*. Prepared by a committee of the National Conference on Research in English. Champaign, Ill.: Council of Teachers of English, c1954.

Carmichael, L. E., *Manual of Child Psychology*, 2nd ed. New York: John Wiley & Sons, 1954.

Dawson, M. A., *Teaching Language in the Grades*. Yonkers, N. Y.: World Book Co., 1951.

Herrick, V. and Jacobs, L., *Children and the Language Arts*. New York: Prentice-Hall, Inc., 1955.

McCarthy, Dorothea, et al., *Factors That Influence Language Growth*. Prepared by a committee for the National Conference on Research in English. Chicago: National Council of Teachers of English, c1953.

National Council of Teachers of English, Commission on the English Curriculum, *Language Arts for Today's Children*. New York: Appleton-Century-Croft, 1954.

Piaget, J., *The Language and Thought of the Child*. New York: Harcourt-Brace & Co., 1932. (o.p.)

Russell, David H. (chairman), et al., *Child Development and the Language Arts*. Prepared by a committee of the National Conference on Research in English. Chicago: National Council of Teachers of English, c1953.

Seegers, J. Conrad (chairman), et al., *Interpreting Language*. Prepared by a committee of the National Conference on Research in English. Chicago: National Council of Teachers of English, c1951.

Strickland, R., *Language Arts for the Elementary School*, 2nd ed. Boston: D. C. Heath & Co., 1951.

Van Riper, C., *Teaching Your Child to Talk*. New York: Harper & Brothers, 1950.

Wagoner, Lovisa C., *The Development of Learning in Young Children*. New York: McGraw-Hill Book Co., c1933.